# The Case for
# Catholic Education

Ryan N.S. Topping

# The Case for
# Catholic Education

Why Parents, Teachers, and Politicians
Should Reclaim the Principles
of Catholic Pedagogy

 Angelico Press

First published in the USA
by Angelico Press
© Ryan N.S. Topping 2015
Foreword © Sr. John Mary Fleming, O.P. 2015
All rights reserved

For information, address:
Angelico Press
4709 Briar Knoll Dr.
Kettering, OH 45429
www.angelicopress.com

ISBN 978-1-62138-145-7 (pbk)
ISBN 978-1-62138-146-4 (ebook)

Cover Image:
*Children of the Sea*, Josef Israëls, Dutch, 1872
Oil on Canvas (courtesy of the Rijks Museum, Amsterdam)
Cover Design: Michael Schrauzer

# CONTENTS

# Further Praise for
## *The Case for Catholic Education*

Ryan Topping is one of today's most exciting and dynamic writers. In his latest book he tackles the crucial subject of education with a delightful lucidity which is both engaged and engaging. This is an accessible and eminently readable book on a topic which no Catholic can afford to ignore.

> —Joseph Pearce, author of *Literary Converts* and Director of the Center for Faith and Culture, Aquinas College, Nashville, TN

Dr. Ryan Topping has once again given us a wise and witty, while also intellectually probing, study of contemporary Catholic Education. *The Case for Catholic Education* will surely play a vital role in reinvigorating the handing-on of essential Catholic truths—truths which still remain in danger of being obscured by contemporary revisionist works. As a Dominican, I appreciate Topping's Thomistic approach and the fact that he infuses his insights with a compelling spirit of personalism befitting the abiding dignity of the human person as "another Christ."

> —Sister Joseph Andrew Bogdanowicz, O.P., Dominican Sisters of Mary, Mother of the Eucharist, Ann Arbor, MI

This short book contains an astonishing wealth of insights and practical suggestions. It is grounded in a deep knowledge of the philosophical and historical dimensions of the topic, and while its style is lively and outspoken, it invites quiet reflection and further study. In fact it contains a series of discussion questions and resources for further reading as appendices. The tone is one of urgency, but also of hope and confidence. You will profit by reading and thinking about this work.

> —Dr. Keith Cassidy, President of Our Lady Seat of Wisdom Academy, Barry's Bay, ON, Canada

# The Case for Catholic Education

Ryan Topping has written an engaging and coherent analysis of the state of Catholic education in North America, which will be useful for teachers in Britain, too. Crucially, he does more than identify the pathologies; he recommends a variety of remedies, drawing on the wisdom of educators both ancient and modern.

> —Dr. Paul Shrimpton, Magdalen College School, Oxford, UK, author of *The 'Making of Men': the Idea and reality of Newman's university in Oxford and Dublin*

As late-born heirs to the tradition of Catholic education, we receive from Ryan Topping an insightful view of our threatened patrimony and a framed vision for what educating and forming our children may still yet become.

> —Dr. Jason Fugikawa, Dean of Academics and Faculty, Holy Family Academy, Manchester, NH

*The Case for Catholic Education* draws on the educational insights of Plato, Aristotle, Augustine, Aquinas, Maritain, Adler and John Senior, *inter alia,* and includes sound advice in regards to the teaching of Good Books and then Great Books in the high school years, and for including Christ throughout an education, without whom schools become like "concrete bunkers with no windows."

> —Patrick S.J. Carmack, Founder of the Angelicum Academy and the Great Books Academy homeschool programs and Executive Director of the Adler-Aquinas Institute, Colorado Springs, CO

Topping makes statistical study, cultural and historical analysis, and pedagogical philosophy come alive with piercing insight, profound wisdom, both actual and parabolic anecdotes, and nearly Chestertonian witticisms. It is impossible to read this book without feeling stirred to the joy—and the work—of better educating our young people.

> —Patrick Conley, Director of Faith Formation, Cathedral of St. Paul, MN

# Further Praise for *The Case for Catholic Education*

In his latest offering, Ryan Topping presents a lucid and lively exploration of the foundations of a true Catholic education. Thoroughly researched and completely accessible, *The Case for Catholic Education* is an engaging and compelling read for anyone interested in the state of Catholic education and the renewal of Catholic culture.

> —Veronica Burchard, Vice President for Education Programs, Sophia Institute for Teachers, Bedford, NH

In *The Case for Catholic Education* Ryan Topping strikes that rarest balance between erudition and clarity. He neither shies away from challenges nor falls prey to despair; rather, he presents a positive vision and practical suggestions in an eminently engaging way. Every Catholic educator and school administer should read and re-read this fine book.

> —Dr. Jason West, President and Academic Dean, Newman Theological College, Edmonton, AB, Canada

The whole art of education comes down to opening windows of wonder. In our day, those windows have been boarded up and forgotten. Dr. Topping's incisive book tears down the shutters, reminding the benighted that there are, indeed, windows and that they are in need of opening. This little book brings hands to the sills. May they be thrown open wide once more.

> —Sean Fitzpatrick, Headmaster, St. Gregory the Great Academy, Scranton, PA

Dr. Topping reminds us that the purpose of education is not merely to fill minds with facts, but rather to inform—and transform—lives with truth. This engaging book combines incisive appraisal and exposition with inspiring encouragement and exhortation. As a wise pedagogue, Dr. Topping does more than explain why happiness and freedom infallibly accompany a life devoted to the truth—he outlines how such a life is learned and lived.

> —Fr. Cajetan Cuddy, O.P., Dominican Province of St. Joseph, New York, NY

3

# The Case for Catholic Education

# Foreword

Ryan Topping's *The Case for Catholic Education* sets out to renew interest in the liberal arts through a clear understanding of the aims of a Catholic education. At first glance, what constitutes the essence of Catholic pedagogy may seem mysterious to parents, teachers, policymakers, and even pastors themselves. However, a deep understanding of the theology, philosophical groundings, and aims of a Catholic education offers the first steps to a truly transforming and life-giving pedagogy.

Topping opens with a history of the crisis in Catholic education. His story focuses on the Enlightenment's turn to progress, technology, and self-fulfillment wrongly understood. With clarity and boldness, Topping argues that much of modern education is a product of bad philosophy. Understanding where education has gone wrong is, of course, crucial to setting matters right. Topping's presentation and explanation of statistical and sociological research help to show that often the modern educational process has failed to shape and form the human person, whose aim includes union with God and eternal life. Whether one is a parent, teacher, or policymaker, knowing how Catholic schools have impacted social and moral behavior in the past versus in the present shows that there is work to be done in the field of Catholic identity. At the same time, Topping points to particular instances of growth and renewal in Catholic education in both Canada and the United States.

According to Ryan Topping, much of this growth and renewal can be traced back to the rediscovery of the sources of Catholic education, figures such as Augustine, Aquinas, and Newman. Topping convincingly describes the method, order, and rationale of the classical liberal arts tradition. Challenging the contemporary emphasis on abstract learning in elementary schools, Topping explains how Catholic education forms the whole child, educating his senses and sensibilities with expert regard for developmental stages.

Above all, *The Case for Catholic Education* stresses the role of parents in discerning the best education for their children. Topping sounds a trumpet call for living the fundamental principle of subsidiarity, a way of keeping matters as local and simple as possible, not passing the buck immediately to the school or to the government. As Paul VI wrote, "Parents must be recognized as the primary and principal educators of their children" (*Gravissimum Educationis* 3). Topping's words here will definitely empower parents and educators alike to cooperate with greater intentionality: "What we ought not to do is to wait for a bureaucratic solution . . . what we need is a rebirth of a thousand Christian communities." Although Topping's bias towards classical education is evident in his presentation, his insistence on the true aims of Catholic education and the primary role of the parent in a child's education are necessary and important reminders for a rediscovery of a truly Catholic education in our time.

*The Case for Catholic Education* speaks to the heart of the debate over whether Catholic education is "worth it." Ryan Topping's eminently colloquial and readable style, at times intertwined with a caustic commentary, sets forth the challenging truths that ground the essence of Catholic education. *The Case for Catholic Education* will prove a spark to conversations about the purpose and practicalities of Cathoolic schools so that upcoming generations can encounter therein the living person of Jesus Christ, who is the center and measure of any true Catholic education.

Sister John Mary Fleming, O.P.
Executive Director for Catholic Education
United States Conference of Catholic Bishops

# Preface

If you wish to bore, try to say everything. In what follows I have said only a few things about the first things of education. These reflections are offered to politicians and administrators, to professional teachers, and, above all, to parents.

Catholic schools in North America have long contributed to the mission of the Church and to the flourishing of society. During the last forty years, however, Catholic schools have suffered severe losses, both in their religious identity and in their ability to attract students. In the previous decade alone, the number of students in American Catholic schools fell by almost twenty percent. As the following pages show, students in Catholic schools these days are more likely to believe in God than public school students, and to be pro-life. At the same time, they more often use marijuana and are, on average, more sexually active. How did this happen? And more importantly, how can we rebuild our schools and reinvigorate our pedagogy?

The recent history of our schools is largely the record of a conflict of loyalties. While many Catholic educators have remained faithful to the Church's vision for education, others have drunk deeply from the wells of secular philosophy. Two generations ago the Catholic view of the human person was abandoned by many educators, and often unintentionally, in favor of alien anthropologies. This turn in theory has led to confusion in practice. In the Christian view, anthropology without theology is apostasy. Forget Christ and dignity disappears. Forget Christ and the solid moral and mental discipline that once characterized Catholic schools is bound to boil down into a soup of good intentions. That broth no longer satisfies. Increasingly, Catholics express a desire to recover a form of education consonant with our dignity. This book aims to encourage that ambition. What it proposes is a set of principles that might guide any genuine renewal of the Catholic culture in our homes and in our institutions. The opening two chapters survey the history and present status of Catholic education in North America. The remaining chapters name and defend principles that once animated our practice and, for the good of our children, should once more be reclaimed.

These first principles are sometimes spoken of as the "causes" of education. These may be divided according to their final, efficient, formal and material senses. Final causes refer to the purposes of learning; efficient causes, to questions of pedagogy; formal and material causes, to the curriculum. My discussion reflects this order. After drawing on historical and sociological research, chapter three takes up the purposes of education; chapter four looks at the methods of the teacher; chapter five, at the liberal arts curriculum. The final chapter points to signs of present renewal.

In the midst of this discussion other important principles emerge. Along the way, and against nationalized curricula, I argue for greater parental responsibility; I uncover the anti-Christian origins of "progressive" education; I show why virtue is more valuable to student learning than is "self-esteem"; I propose the liberal arts as the best foundation for a "common core" curriculum; I explain why traditional educators encourage imitation before creative self-expression. In making my case for a retrieval of these principles, I draw from the greatest philosophers of the Christian tradition, from Church documents, as well as from statistical and anecdotal evidence.

Two other features of this work are worth noting. The first is that I have included questions and a research guide in two appendixes. My hope is that this work might inspire curiosity and spur discussion. The second is that this book is best read alongside another. I have had the joy of editing a companion volume, *Renewing the Mind: A Reader in the Philosophy of Catholic Education*, with a foreword by Don J. Briel (Catholic University of America Press, 2015); those wishing to delve further into the rich sources of the Catholic tradition of thinking about learning might find something of interest in those pages.

The seeds of several chapters of this book first appeared in a series on Catholic education in *Catholic Insight Magazine*. I am grateful to its editor, David Beresford, for permission to incorporate elements of those articles here. My wife, Anna Topping, provided helpful criticisms of the text. I thank Sr. John Mary Fleming for her gracious foreword and for her thoughtful comments on an earlier draft of this book. Finally, I offer thanks to John Riess as well as the staff at Angelico Press, and to the parents, religious, and other educators who have shown support for this project.

Jesus said we will always have the poor. These days, the poverty that most afflicts us is of the heart and of the spirit. This is where Catholic educators can serve the mission of the Church. Pope Benedict XVI memorably said that before all else the school is "a place to encounter the living God." This reflects a lofty ambition. I dedicate these reflections to those teachers who would translate this promise into a living experience.

Thomas More College, New Hampshire
Feast of St. Monica, 2015

*Madonna of Humility*, Fra Angelico

# 1

# The Crisis of Catholic Education: A History with a Lesson

Defending education feels a little bit like defending spring. Who could argue against fresh air and sunshine? Yet we have grown accustomed to frost. And so the defence of education, at least one noble conception of it, is what the day demands. I wish to open these essays on the principles of Catholic education by sketching our need for their recovery, by offering a history with a lesson. Beyond the obligation to secure funding, to reduce class sizes, and to produce well-trained teachers—conditions necessary for the health of all schools—is the need to renew our understanding. The crisis of Catholic education, which the next generation of students and teachers must overcome, is a crisis born chiefly of our lack of confidence in truth. This lack of confidence has led us to accept an uninspired and uninspiring view of the human person.

I begin by noting observations made two generations ago. Already in 1961 the eminent English convert and Harvard historian Christopher Dawson (1889–1970) identified the cultural conditions which undermine our practice of teaching and learning in his seminal work, the *Crisis of Western Education*.[1] The malaise that afflicts the West, so he argued, has two components. The first is directly intellectual. Since Immanuel Kant's rejection of metaphysics and our now-habitual reliance upon technology as a pseudo-

13

substitute for religion, confidence in reason has dried up. Reason still has a place. But it no longer serves, so we imagine, as an instrument for knowing ultimate truths. For us, only empirical observations count. Nature cannot teach us about what is good. This positivistic conception of reason is a macabre image of our own creating. It is an edifice at once gruesome and arid, which Benedict XVI likened in one of his finest speeches to "a concrete bunker with no windows";[2] and it suffocates. It suffocates because it crushes the moral imagination; it stifles because it arbitrarily narrows the range within which modern man is willing to think about thinking. Thus, instead of openness to wonder, openness to beauty, to truth, goodness, angels, eternity, the music of the spheres, the soul, and the like, the scope of reason is reduced to aims dictated largely by the economy and the imperatives of technological innovation, to computer chips and airplanes.

*"In its self-proclaimed exclusivity the positivist reason which recognizes nothing beyond mere functionality resembles a concrete bunker with no windows. . . ."*—Benedict XVI, "Address to the German Parliament," September 22, 2011

A dozen examples from the daily news could illustrate. Here is one. Recently, criticism has been leveled against the "Common Core Standards" initiative, now adopted by some 46 American states, and which will surely be approved by countless Catholic and charter schools. Most would agree that the intention behind the Common Core effort is laudable. Public education in the U.S. is poor. American students lag behind kids from other industrialized nations. On standardized tests, at age 15, Americans rank 27th in science and only a bit better in reading, at 24th (that's one up from the Czech Republic).[3]

While social conservatives may be more likely to protest this initiative, the Common Core represents, in some way, the culmination of the standards movement. Conservative opinion of the previous generation gathered around the 1983 Department of Education's landmark publication of *A Nation at Risk*. That document was the first to identify the deleterious effects of "cafeteria curricula" upon students; it was also the first to generate wide-spread doubt as to whether America should continue the long slide toward vocational and therapeutic education.

Still, not everyone is cheering. Some have objected to the federal government's functional imposition of a national curriculum; others wonder about the wisdom of adopting nation-wide standards that have not yet been field-tested; still others disagree with the content and structure mandated, for instance, the stipulation that 70% of a high-school senior's reading must be "informational" as opposed to "literary."[4] I wish to speak to none of these concerns. Whatever else may be said for or against the project, I observe only that its aims are brutally utilitarian. Its founding document makes this plain: the Core exists to "ensure that all students are college and career ready in literacy no later than the end of high school." Is that all for which we can hope?

The Common Core is a reasonable document. Its influence will extend well beyond the United States. It was composed, we are told, after wide consultation. And who could not wish that, at the end of thirteen years of institutional discipline, paid at public expense, all students would be employable? The problem with the document is not that it is wicked but that it is banal. Thomas Gradgrind, that dreary caricature of a functionary head-master in Charles

Dickens' *Hard Times*, comes to look every day more like a visionary when set beside our educational experts. The interesting question to ask is not whether 13 years of industrial education will equip a child to feed himself. The interesting question to ask is whether we will have supplied him with a reason to live. And for that matter: what is a good life? Students, we suppose, will learn eventually how to fill in that blank.

To educate, from the Latin *educo*, means to draw out. To teach a child is to "pull out" of their nature some things and to leave behind others. The Common Core document, and others like it, presumes that in our public speech we should not raise, let alone attempt to answer, the ultimate justifications for education that make success in college and career worthwhile goals to pursue. Mark this: clever students note the absence. To educate is to act. And to act is to move on the basis of some precept stated or implied. To refuse to answer the question of ultimate ends is itself to supply a certain answer. In our time, public reason can deliver the iPhone but must play deaf to the aims of sex, to the meaning of life, and even, as it appears, to the reasons for literature. Our educational objectives and methods proceed accordingly. From the nursery to the university, our schools promote at once two opposing and mutually destructive tendencies: vocationalism and hyper-specialization. What has been lost from view even within Catholic schools is a sense of the unifying vision of a liberal education.

A distinction is in order. In a democratic society all students must read, write, and, if they are to survive in a market economy, compute. The three Rs fulfill this just political ambition. But education has aims that are supra-political. We don't educate our children simply so that they will become good citizens, or good capitalists. Before they are our charge, they are God's children. Each child carries dual citizenship. Man requires bread. The Good Samaritan needed coins in his pocket to offer some; it is proper that we teach kids how to find them. But we need more than bread. Far more important is the good we do with however little or much we make. From this twofold necessity arises the two classes of education. Where *servile* education focuses only on the means of life, *liberal* education considers also the ends of life. We need skilled carpenters, accountants, and nurses. But before anyone is a good house-builder, he ought to be a good man.

Liberal education, then, aims to teach a man or a woman how to be good. Since the Greeks, the seven liberal arts—grammar, logic, rhetoric, geometry, arithmetic, astronomy, music—have been enlisted as the formal means in the service of this ambition. It was defined first by Plato and Aristotle, extended by Augustine, and applied by medieval and Renaissance humanists. The nature and shape of liberal education was commonly understood in the West up through the 19th century. In recent times, Dorothy Sayers's essay "The Lost Tools of Learning" has served as a marvelous introduction to this tradition.[5]

> *"Instruction in the liberal arts produces devotees more alert and steadfast and better equipped for embracing truth. . . ."*—St. Augustine, *On Order* (1.8.24)

If the first aspect of this crisis undermines the intellect, the second impoverishes the imagination. This other failure perpetuated by contemporary education is the loss of contact with our past, specifically Christianity's contribution to the West. Simply as a point of fact, apart from the martyrs, the monks, the crusaders, the schoolmen, and the missionaries, and apart from the Mass, there would have been no such thing as "the West." Dawson's prescient achievement nearly half-a-century ago was to see that not only is faith disappearing; history, too, is receding from our view, and with it, a living connection to our cultural roots. It is the loss of contact with our spiritual and cultural legacy, so Dawson warned, that accounts for our contemporary rootlessness. We believe in rights, but have no idea from whence they came; we preach free speech, but jail politically incorrect ministers.

We want tolerance without truth. This hole in our heart has made us prey to a string of violent and bizarre fanaticisms, from the French revolution, to the Fascist and Communist revolutions, to the sexual and jihadist revolutions now upon us. As the international regime of *Human Rights Commissions* proves—or the fact that high-profile CEOs can now be bullied out of their positions for supporting traditional marriage—such tolerance turns out to be tyrannical.[6] We are what Nietzsche called the "last men": agnostic moralists, fueled by righteous indignation, guided by irreligious conviction. Without a recovery of the sources of Christian culture, the art, history, and institutions that shaped us, Western technological man will find no way of saving himself from degrading servitude, if not to despots, then to his own passions.

Dawson's solution was suggestive. He advocated not so much a return to the Great Books (though these must play a role in any rescue of modern education) as a return, more broadly, to the study of that culture out of which the Great Books themselves were formed. The problem, as he described it, is not so much that we are anti-religious. The problem is that we have made ourselves sub-religious—a condition which is also sub-human. The best means to reawaken our contemporaries, he thought, was an histori-cally-inspired, religiously-informed rebirth of Catholic liberal education.

Since the 1960's, evidence of the crisis described by Dawson has only mounted. Even if one disagrees with Dawson's practical recommenda-tions, the effects of the breakdown in the mental and moral discipline of Catholic schools and colleges are hard to miss. My focus is on the education of

*"To perform its teaching and research functions effectively the Catholic university must have true autonomy and academic freedom in the face of authority of whatever kind, lay or clerical, external to the academic community itself."*— 1967 *Land O'Lakes Statement* by (rogue) Catholic College Presidents

teens, roughly from the ages of 13 to 21. Because it is cus-tomary to divide high school sharply from college, throughout I'll focus more on the early years of liberal edu-cation. Here let me only mention a few signs of the loss of a Catholic ethos in colleges.

In 1967 leading dissident Catholic university presidents signed a manifesto known as the *Land O'Lakes Statement*. The text formally declared their independence from the institutional Church. A widely cited study of the belief and behavior of students at U.S. Catholic colleges quantified the consequences then set in motion: 31% of students now become more supportive of legalized abortion after their years at college (whereas 16% become more pro-life); 32% decrease their Mass attendance (whereas 7% increase it);

54% of students say that their experience of attending a Catholic college has no effect on their support for Catholic teachings.[7] The situation in Canada is worse. At the time of the Second Vatican Council (1962–1965), Canadians attended church more often than did Americans, and could boast of a broad network of Catholic colleges—some 57, not counting those inside Quebec. In the fifteen years after the Council that network unravelled. By the early 1980's two out of three Catholic colleges had closed or been absorbed by the provincial universities. Presently, only a few colleges even claim to offer something of an integrated Catholic formation.

Any sharp divide between high school and undergraduate formation is arbitrary. Decay in the identity of colleges is bound to affect the lower schools. When we lost the universities, Catholic high schools also lost somewhere to send their best kids, and along with this, they seem to have lost something of their own core identity. Think of it this way. Education is like sport. When you lose your major leagues, the best athletes have nowhere to go, and your minor leagues have nowhere to send them. When the identity of universities collapsed, Catholics lost their major leagues. And so, the minors became just a bit less serious about their task of evangelizing students, of forming them in the Christian intellectual tradition.

What is to be done? What we ought not to do is to wait for a bureaucratic solution. The problem is not even that we need more money, though endowments indeed must grow. The source of our crisis is in the mind, and in the heart. What we need is a rebirth of a thousand Christian communities, and among them a renewed understanding of and loyalty to the principles of learning that have animated our tradition for centuries. What we need in our homes and in our schools is to welcome a new springtime of Catholic education. Even now the days grow brighter. But before I propose principles of renewal, our first task will be to survey the craters on the landscape.

*The School Walk*, David Cox

# 2

# The Schools and Our Children:
# No Passing Grade

How healthy are the schools and our children? We'll look at the curriculum shortly. For a long time already parents have recognized that the gravest weakness of Catholic schools is not in their incapacity to pass along the three Rs. Where they have failed is in teaching the faith. As has become plain, despite our millions of dollars invested in teachers and technologies, we apparently can't even convince students that there is such a thing as objective moral truth. It's not only the parents who've taken notice. Listen to what St. John Paul II not long ago said of Catholic schools in America:

> The greatest challenge to Catholic education in the United States today, and the greatest contribution that authentically Catholic education can make to American culture, is to restore to that culture the conviction that human beings can grasp the truth of things, and, in grasping that truth, can know their duties to God, to themselves and their neighbors.[8]

For a snapshot of our teens we'll rely chiefly upon recent national surveys as well as the work of two of North America's most eminent sociologists, Reginald Bibby and Christian Smith. After thirty years of industrial education, the fact that teens in North America substantially share the same likes and dislikes ought not to surprise. What shocks is how little difference it makes to their sentiments—in most cases—whether a child is studying at a Catholic or a public school.

⊕

Let's begin with the schools in the United States. Currently, there are some 6,568 Catholic schools in America (among them 1,200 high schools), educating just under two million students. Catholic schools have an illustrious history in the United States. The first was opened by the Franciscans in St. Augustine, Florida, in 1606. The Jesuits began their missions along the Great Lakes in 1632, where they translated Huron into a written script and then taught their hosts how to read. In the East, John Carroll established Georgetown in 1789 around the same time St. Junipero Serra labored among the Indians along the West coast, not long before Elizabeth Ann Seton opened St. Joseph's Academy for girls in Emmetsburg, Maryland. It was during the second half of the 19th century, however, that America experienced the greatest influx of European Catholics. It was this second wave of arrivals that prepared the way for the subsequent expansion. In 1900 America was home to ten million Catholics, supporting 3,500 parochial schools. This number nearly doubled by the end of the First World War. At the height of the parochial system, during the mid-1960's, Catholic elementary and secondary schools enrolled five-and-a-half million students.

The decline was swift. During the 1970's and 1980's, the number of students dropped by more than half, even while the Catholic population was growing. Although new growth among Catholic schools has begun, unfortunately, the overall slide continues. In the ten years after 2005, for instance, the number of students declined by 481,016, or 19% of the student population. Currently, just under two million students are enrolled in Catholic schools. Last year 27 new schools opened, while 88 consolidated or closed. The most dramatic decreases have been in major urban dioceses, and especially along the Boston-Washington corridor. These figures are seen best in context. Though the Catholic population has more than tripled since 1930, there are now fewer students in American Catholic schools than there were nearly one century ago. A mere 15 out of every 100 Catholic teens currently study in a Catholic school. No longer is the local parish school the default preference for faithful parents. In fact, today slightly more children are educated at home than in Catholic schools.

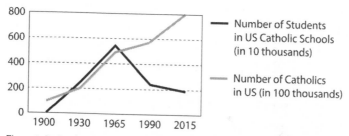

**Figure 1:** Ratio of students to US Catholic Population (Sources: NCEA, CARA, etc.)

Bishops still support the schools. Official publications hail Catholic schools as serving the Church's mission in a "vital" role.[11] They do so with good reason. As history both ancient and modern attests, the first site of cultural conflict is the classroom. After all, he who runs schools today, rules tomorrow. The loss in the sheer number of institutions, to say nothing of their ethos, has hindered the Church's evangelical reach. No youth, no future. Christian teens everywhere face the same trials: the failing marriages of their parents, the break-up of civic decency, pimples. Yet young Catholics seem particularly unprepared.

Consider a few comparisons. According to the *National Survey of Youth and Religion* (NSYR), when it comes to metaphysics, a solid 85% of Catholic teens (13–17 years old) believe in a First Cause. About two out of three even think it thinks! Get more specific, however, and their views become cloudy. Just over half believe in angels, or that God can work miracles. That's ahead of the un-churched kids, but far behind the Evangelicals (79% of whom believe in angels, and 77% in miracles). One out of four prays daily. One out of three has fasted at least once this past year—about the same number that might consult their horoscope before buying a car.[12]

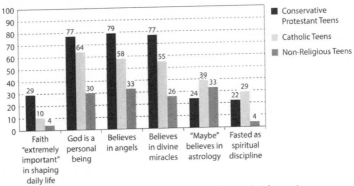

**Figure 2**: Religious beliefs among teens (Source: Smith, 2005)

Catholic baby boomers often complain about the Church's strict sex code. The kids seem not to have heard of it. A scene from Walker Percy's *The Moviegoer* comes to mind. Binx Bolling is a stockbroker and lapsed Catholic from the South who while in search of his soul has surrendered himself to Aphrodite. He is travelling by train from

New Orleans to Chicago with an old love. They've suffered a failed attempt at intimacy, and, after the affair, he is left to his own reflections. Not even flesh pleases:

> What a sickness it is, Rory, this latter-day post-Christian sex. To be pagan it would be one thing, an easement taken easily in a rosy old pagan world; to be Christian it would be another thing, fornication forbidden and not even to be thought of in the new life, and I can see that it need not be thought of if there were such a life. But to be neither pagan nor Christian but this: oh this is sickness, Rory. . . .[13]

It's a sickness now spread far and wide. One diocese recently sponsored a comprehensive study aiming to measure the effect of sex education on teens. The study tested several hundred high-school seniors, 79% of whom attended one of eight local Catholic high schools—the remaining were enrolled in parish religious-education programs. Nearly all students surveyed were Catholic. Here are a few of the results: 22% said they hoped to save sex for marriage; 72% said they would be willing to have intercourse if they were in "a serious relationship"; one out of two had visited a sex chat room on the internet; 55% had engaged in oral sex, 42% in intercourse; and 29% abstained from both activities as well as onanism. America is vast, but what this diocese found fits well within the national picture.[14] According to national studies, just under half of Catholic teens are virgins and hope to remain so till marriage, and a mere 11% agree strongly that contraception is wrong.[15]

Compared with Evangelicals, Catholic teens think less like Christians and behave more like the unbaptized. Why this difference? For one thing, Evangelical Protestant churches make a larger investment in youth ministry. Only

12% of Catholic teens participate in a religious youth group, as opposed to 23–43% of Protestants. If you're a Baptist, chances are high that your congregation pays for a youth pastor: between 81% and 86% of Protestant teens attend a church with a youth group. By contrast, only 2 out of 3 Catholic youth worship at a parish that has organized such a ministry.[16] At the level of infrastructure, Catholics simply haven't caught up. For most of the 20th century, Catholic identity was bound together by a three-strand rope: the family, the parish, and the school. The first two cords have weathered, so the weight now hangs on the third.

It is sometimes trumpeted that youth these days have no interest in religion. That is not true. They have simply rejected its traditional form. At the conclusion of a nat-

> *"Public subsidies [ought to] be paid out in such a way that parents are truly free to choose according to their conscience the schools they want for their children."* — Vatican Two Declaration on Education, *Gravissimum Educationis*, §6

ional study of the religious practices of 3,300 teens, Christian Smith considers just what is replacing Christianity. It's not atheism. It's not even hip-hop hedonism. When it comes to fundamental beliefs, the kids generally shuffle behind their parents, wherever it is they lead them. Where they're being led just happens to look more like Disneyland than Lourdes. What is displacing traditional belief in North America is not Islam but what Smith calls a new faith: Moralistic, Therapeutic Deism. It's a religion like any other, except that it happens to be soft on doctrine, rich in psychology, and, above all, high on tolerance. And the description fits pretty well across the continent.

# The Schools and Our Children: No Passing Grade

⊕

For another look at the problem, I'd like to turn for a moment to the North. Catholics in the United States may attend Mass more often, but for historical reasons, Canadians have access to a greater number of Catholic schools.[17] Closer to European models, Catholic education in Canada has traditionally been funded by the state. Some 5 million students are enrolled in K–12 education; nearly 1 in 5 teens (some 340,000) has his or her desk in a Catholic high school.[18] Now, as a matter of established doctrine, Catholics insist that a government which taxes parents incurs the duty to help fund their children's education. Certainly, along the lines of the Second Vatican Council, parents should state their case: we believe that "public subsidies [ought to] be paid out in such a way that parents are truly free to choose according to their conscience the schools they want for their children."[19] Of course, you sometimes hear a parent say, "let the unions fend for themselves, and the money follow the child!" But let the buyer beware: in our culture, cash comes at a high cost.

We'll walk through the details, but here's the conclusion. When we ask whether it will make much difference if we send our teen to a state-funded public or to a state-funded Catholic high school in Canada, the answer is *not much*. On the matter of belief, and personal morals, it's not that the kids in the two main publicly-funded systems are wicked. They're actually pretty nice. What the research shows is that they mostly cherish the same virtues, aspire to the same goals, and engage in the same behaviors. Similar to the research from the United States, what is discouraging about the character of Canadian teens educated by the

Church is not so much their badness; what depresses is their moral mediocrity.

Teens in public and Catholic schools love the same things. Both kinds of students list as "very important" the virtues of trust (84%/85%) and honesty (81%/85%). Collectively, the kids are downright polite—about half say you should not give someone the finger! They know what decency looks like in a tolerant society: 94% of the 15–19-year-olds say everyone is entitled to free medical care; 82% disapprove of parking in a handicapped stall when you're not really handicapped. Fewer get up for church: 67% attend "hardly ever" or "never," though a solid 21% worship every week—we'll come back to this minority.[20] Prayer may be illegal in the public system, but at least everyone is against bullying. In short, most teens are nice. And by all accounts, most schools are doing a fine job keeping them that way.

Today's students may be friendly. This does not mean you'd want to hire just any summer-student to shingle your roof. Nor can you trust a majority of them with your change. If you can believe it, when researchers asked thousands of teens across the country whether they think "right and wrong is a matter of personal opinion," 64% said they did; in the United States, that rises in some studies to 83%.[21] But let's stay with the modest figures. Some two out of three teens say morals are relative. Relative to what? Relative not to some external standard but to how they happen to *feel*.

Apparently, the kids mean what they say. If morals are relative, what's so bad about theft? When asked the question, "would you return a $10 bill that was overpaid to you by a cashier," about the same number of teens in the Canadian study (roughly 6 out of 10) either said they would keep the bill and keep trucking, or that it "would depend." Depend on what, you ask? Perhaps whether you looked like the kind of cashier who hides a bat under the till? Or, maybe, whether they thought they would like a second bag of Cheesy Nachos on the way back from the beach? Who's to judge? If you're merely nice, nobody's to judge.

That's the problem. Our schools are filled with young people who've been told that the one really big sin in the world is to judge somebody's character—especially their own. The majority of today's teens are nice. And it's not really their fault. Most of them for years have been subjected to the schools' falsely conceived "self-esteem regime."

It is a fact not often reported, but enhanced self-esteem can damage a student's chances for success—especially if it is not grounded in reality. An OECD (*Organization of Economic Co-Operation and Development*) global study, for instance, recently asked pupils around the world how well they thought they did in mathematics. 77% of American students thought they earned "good grades in mathematics" (up from 72% about a decade previously). This compared to 58% of Finns, and 33% in Hong Kong.[22] And how well do they in fact know their numbers? Among the world's fifteen-year-olds, students from Hong Kong placed 3rd while those from the United States ranked 36th.[23] Contrary to the conclusions of popular psychology, what this international study suggests is an inverse relationship between self-esteem and actual achievement.

In any case, students may be struggling with math, but they've grasped the philosophy of no-fault living. "Whatever you do—you're still OK." It's a friendly philosophy at heart. The reasoning goes, if we fail Johnny, or tell him that what he's doing on the weekend is a little creepy, we might hurt his self-esteem. That's true. To be told you're not working hard enough, or that you're not mature enough, can hurt. To our shame, however, public and Catholic schools alike too often draw the wrong conclusion. Instead of showing our children how obstacles can build character, and how failure can point to our need for redemption, what we've sometimes allowed our kids to believe is that you can succeed even if you don't try hard.

I do not imply that every fault in a child is the responsibility of their school. The school, of course, is not the only agent working to shape our children. Hollywood, Beyoncé, and Pepsi Cola annually dedicate billions of dollars to enticing our children to "live for now."[24] Good teachers must daily contend against the Goliaths who rule the media. Unfortunately, whether we approve of the messages being lobbed at our children or not, many of them are taking home the wrong lessons. In Canada one thing a lot of students in both public and Catholic schools say is that they don't like *hard work*. When asked whether hard work was a quality they valued highly, only 56% of the public school kids ticked the box, compared to 58% from the Catholic system. They say this while eight out of ten claim they expect to make more money than their parents. Less work, more pay? The disconnect between what they imagine and what awaits them breaks the heart.

To conclude this survey, I'd like to shift our focus from quantitative to qualitative research. Let me break down the differences between kids in public and Canadian Catholic (as well as private Christian) schools under three headings: what they want; what they believe; what they do. Figure three compares our students' aspirations regarding education, work, and romance.

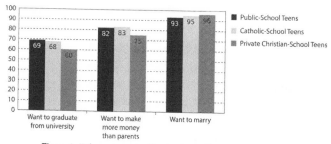

Figure 3: What teens want for the future (Source: Bibby, 2009)

On their wants, so far, so similar. The only difference of statistical note is that youths in private schools normally have a better grasp of the dynamics of the economy. As we'll see next, they also have a better sense of what makes for success in love and marriage.

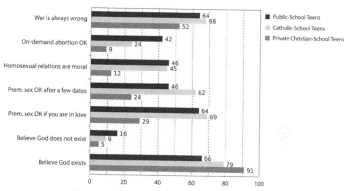

Figure 4: What teens believe (Source: Bibby, 2009)

A solid majority of public and catholic school kids think that premarital sex is OK as long as "you are in love with the person." By college a lot of these youngsters will start shacking up together. This is a pity. We saw above that almost everyone also wants to get married—and presumably stay married. Here is another instance where a permissive ethic has led to painful results.

Whether or not teens believe in the philosophy of *Alice in Wonderland*, it's up to us to shepherd them into adulthood. In real life there are a few standard goal posts. Kick at them if you like. It's the child's toe that is going to break, or his heart.

Teenagers love to argue. And we should be willing to meet them on this ground. Appeals to the authority of the Church can be helpful. But what teens need, above all, is to see the rationale behind the rules. I can imagine a high school teacher offering just such a response to a sixteen-year-old who wanted to know why he shouldn't live with his girlfriend before marriage.

Student: Mr. Peters...

Teacher: Yes, Mr. Sampson.

Student: I've been thinking about your lesson on the "theology of the body."

Teacher: I'm glad. What did you think of it?

Student: It was, well, interesting.

Teacher: How interesting...

Student: Yes, well, I've got a few questions I wanted to ask you.

Teacher: Fire away.

Student: A couple of my friends and I were talking after class. And we're not sure if what you said about chastity makes sense. You test drive cars; why wouldn't a couple... you know... test their compatibility before getting married?

Teacher: Yes, I do know. Good question...

[*Thoughtfully timed pause*]

Teacher: Do you have your iPhone on you?

Student: Pardon?

Teacher: Your iPhone. Is it working?

Student: Oh yes, I... I don't understand.

Teacher: I know. Do you hope to get married?

Student: Sure, one day.

Teacher: Alright. Presumably, you'll also want to stay married. Let's Google some stats.

Student: Uh, Mr. Peters...

Teacher: Yes.

Student: I'm sorry. My internet's down, can we use yours?

Teacher: Here's a better idea. I'm going to give you an assignment. It won't take long. And it might make you happy. Up for it?

Student: Well, alright.

Teacher: When you get home I'd like you to Google "Stats on Marriage." Click on the first hit you see. Bring to tomorrow's class a one-page report on what you find... and we'll debate it.

Student: OK. I like our debates.

Teacher: Me too...

Mr. Peters is a wise teacher. He knows what his student will bring to their next religion class after only a little digging; among the statistics readily available, his student will discover:

- For the lads: if they live with their girlfriend, they are twice as likely to divorce than if they hadn't;
- For the lassies: women who live with a common-law partner are about three times more likely to suffer abuse than are real wives;

- For their kids: children of divorced couples experience poorer grades, worse health, and less stability in their own relationships;
- Married men are healthier and make more money than unmarried men; the most financially, socially, and psychologically secure place a woman can find herself is in a marriage;[25]
- The largest impoverished demographic is *single mothers*... etc.[26]

Statistics alone aren't likely to change a student's heart. But they can incite thought. Even more, they help show that the Church's doctrines related to romance are based not merely on authority, but on sound reason. Virtue serves our own best interests.

At this point I'd like to anticipate a reasonable objection. Some might wonder whether the weakened religious identity of our schools is due to the presence of non-Catholics. Maybe. I note that these days, two out of three kids in Canadian Catholic schools still report that they are Catholic. That is down from 85% in 1984 (where it stands today in American Catholic schools), but Catholics remain a strong majority. A more likely explanation is simply that the "inside" of a parish community looks a lot more like the "outside" than it did a generation ago. As we saw above, one bright spot for the children in Catholic schools is that they are less likely to believe in the goodness of abortion on demand. This is an achievement worth celebrating. Those who work in Catholic schools should be congratulated and seek to build from this strength.

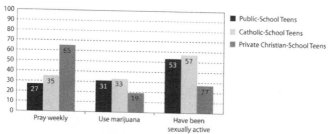

**Figure 5:** What teens do (Source: Bibby, 2009)

Lastly, what do teens do? Figures four and five provide a rough sketch. Kids in Catholic schools are much more likely to believe in God; they pray more often than the public school students. These same youth, however, also fornicate and hallucinate more than everybody else. In terms of comparable beliefs, once you catch the pattern, you can see how much the kids are alike—or, as we shall see, unlike.

In sum, there is both good and bad news. The bad news is that, on both quantitative and qualitative measures, in the post-Vatican Two era children have graduated from our schools largely unevangelized. The good news is that clarity has now begun to return. Less and less are parents (and pastors for that matter) willing to tolerate institutions that undermine the faith of our children. As to the future, we Catholics will need to learn how to rebuild our institutions in the midst of a culture that has turned hostile to our faith; we will need to recover confidence in our creed; and we will need to reclaim the principles of our practice.

To begin this work of reclamation, we return to that most basic question: Why study?

*St. Jerome in His Study*, Albrecht Dürer

# 3

# The Purposes of Education:
# Happiness, Culture, Virtue

Why set the alarm when friends sleep in? Even if a father might not ask why he should work, his son is very likely to ask why he ought to study. Consider the father's potential replies. He might answer: so that his son can pass his exams; or so that he can enter college; or so that he can eventually earn a living. And—retorts the teenage boy— why should I want a job! As even five minutes with an enquiring adolescent will make plain, the very notion of a final cause or purpose can be distinguished. Armed with faith and a basic grounding in philosophy, I suggest this is how the father ought to answer: first, the son should study because it can contribute to his own everlasting happiness (the ultimate purpose); second, it will improve his culture (the remote purpose); third, it will perfect his virtue or skill (the immediate purpose). Happiness, culture, and virtue thus correspond to the three pur-poses of Catholic education.[27]

I wish to focus on the ultimate purpose, and on the culture of the school. This is not because pre-

> *The ends of education are threefold: happiness, culture and virtue.*

paring a child for a fulfilling career is unimportant. It's just that everybody already values good jobs. What is more, Catholic schools have long raised a disproportionate num-ber of children out of poverty, and prepared those from every background for college.[28] Then again, perhaps not everybody is familiar with these achievements.

Merely from an economic point of view, Catholic schools provide an enormous service to our communities. I will offer figures from just one region. Pennsylvania's Catholics make up about 23% of their state's population. These three million Catholics currently support some 500 Catholic schools, educating some 150,000 young people. In Pennsylvania, taxpayers dole out about $15,000 for each child who warms a desk in a public school. The education of tens of thousands of students is paid from other purses because of the faith of Catholic parents in their own schools. The public savings? 2.28 billion dollars. That's a lot of money that the parents and teachers who support Sacred Heart School in Lancaster, PA, and others like it around the state, had to find elsewhere.[29] In the face of the unjust economic disadvantages that private schools face, the academic success of Catholic schools around the country is no mean achievement.

And yet we can do better. Indeed, if we don't improve our sense of mission, the sacrifices that sustain our schools will soon not be worth the effort. While our schools have maintained a high level of academic achievement, where we have failed is in transmitting convincingly a Christian vision of man's ultimate end, of the nature of happiness. Let us be clear on this point. Debates over pedagogy, curricula, and educational "outcomes" presume some prior conception of the goal of man's striving. It is here, at the place where theology and anthropology intersect, that Catholic educators must relearn how to restate their case. What makes a Catholic school worth fighting for is not simply the freedom to hang a crucifix over the front entrance—though that too is important. What is at stake in the battles over the curriculum reflects a much deeper conflict. Between a genuinely Catholic school and its secular counterpart lies a disagreement over two conceptions of the purposes of education, two conceptions of the goal of human freedom. Where the Church proclaims a *freedom for excellence*, the prevailing secular view defends merely man's *freedom of expression*—the view of freedom that, as it happens, also lies at the root of the 20th-century movement of "progressive" education.

Let's begin with the reigning secular view of freedom, and its remote Christian origins. Before we launch into this history I offer one note. One of the reasons so-called "progressive education" became attractive to educators is because it mimics features of Christian belief. In its original manifestations, it celebrated the individual; it emphasized conscience and the virtue of authenticity; it seemed, above all, to offer a new increase for freedom. The traditional and the progressive systems of pedagogy indeed at points look similar; yet it would be a mistake to confuse them. Progressive education in its classic form diametrically opposes the Christian view. As we'll see over the next two chapters, whether you celebrate the Church's account of *freedom for excellence* or progressive educators' *freedom of expression* will determine how you answer numerous secondary questions about the goals of learning, the nature of the curriculum, and your favored techniques of pedagogy. Those educators who wish to arm themselves for the future fight for Catholic education would therefore do well to turn to this history.

During the European Enlightenment, stress was laid on the categorical nature of man's freedom. Without freedom of speech, of association, and above all, of religion, so it was argued, man's dignity suffers. In religion, only a *sincere* faith was deemed defensible. Conscience gained a new credibility. This focus on the interiority of the act of faith was, in certain respects, laudable. There is even Scriptural warrant behind the appeal: St. Paul says, "Let love be sincere" (Rom. 12:9). The Greek word behind the adjective is *anupokritos.* The term means "without hypocrisy." Surely, to be good one must be genuine; but even love added to sincerity forms only a two-legged table. To lean on a table of sincerity and love without the support of its third leg, truth, will lead you, and all your guests, crashing to the floor. As the narrator in Oliver Goldsmith's novel *The Vicar of Wakefield* (1766) wryly puts it, conscience is a true but unsteady guide:

> Conscience is a coward; and those faults it has not strength enough to prevent, it seldom has justice enough to accuse.[30]

As love must be sincere, so must conscience be rooted in truth. John Henry Cardinal Newman (1801–1890) would echo the same sentiment a century later in his *Letter to the Duke of Norfolk:* "Conscience has rights," he explains, "because it has duties."[31] Conscience bears witness to norms. It does not generate them.

In any case, already by Newman's time philosophy on all sides of the Atlantic had long been sailing on the high seas of religious indifference, unloosed from the anchor of the creed. Along with this new emphasis on freedom of conscience came a loss of confidence in man's ability to know the good. 19ᵗʰ-century liberals wished, laudably, to defend conscience. Unfortunately, along the way, conscience was separated from philosophy, common sense, and religion. Armed merely with his interiority, the individual was set to sea on a starless voyage. When conscience lost truth for its rudder, each man was made captain of his own Titanic.

Other consequences followed. At the level of politics and culture, liberty came to mean little more than the absence of external restraint. In effect, the English political philosopher John Stuart Mill (1806–1873) raised the philosophy of brawny eighteen-year-old males to the level of principle. As he asserted in *On Liberty*, a man's "independence is, of right, absolute." So long as one man does not directly harm another, he declared, "the individual is sovereign."[32] I take this to be a good example of *freedom of expression*. Mill's view elevates the act of choice without judging the quality of the act or the object upon which it is exercised. Moderns are destined to be pro-choice.

The new, negatively defined freedom has reordered both politics and education. On the level of theory, the task of political authority came to be seen as defending diversity. All views were to be welcomed except, well, unwelcoming views. On such a foundation, it was only a matter of time before the tolerant state would take on the tactics of a bully.

One need not look far to see how theory has been transformed into policy. After a protracted battle against parents, recently the Ontario provincial government enacted Bill 13, which demands that all schools—including Catholic schools—cooperate in the establishment of "Gay-Straight Alliance Clubs" for children. The mandated clubs were sold as "anti-bullying" measures. In the name of "tolerance," Catholic schools were coerced to act against their own teaching on human sexuality; in the name of "diversity" the ministry for education enforced a dull uniformity. In short, the fantasy of negative freedom has been purchased at a high cost. As transcendence recedes, man does not give up on ideals. When we turn away from God, we do not abandon heaven; we simply try to bring it down to earth. The modern secularist may be irreligious, but he remains piously idealistic. Today, the tolerant are tough on intolerance. Let the buyer beware.

We can contrast this view with that of the Church. Christian faith promotes *freedom for excellence*. Catholics hold that man is capable of reading off of nature norms to direct our behavior. Freedom is a gift; it also carries responsibilities. It is only through the virtues, only by acting in accord with our nature, that man can perfect himself. As the *Catechism* puts it, aided by grace, the virtues "forge character and give facility in the practice of the good" (CCC 1810). Hence, by wisdom a man can perfect his intelligence, by courage his will, by temperance his passions. Not that the project can ever be fully completed in this life. But we make a start. And a truly liberal education will help teach a child where to direct his efforts.

From this review of the two competing accounts of freedom I wish to highlight this unbending rule: conflicts in philosophy lead to conflicts over education. Does freedom have an end? Is man a complicated monkey or merely a dull angel? Is reason reliable? From such questions there is no quiet exit. Education involves a teacher in the formation of the child. Therefore, where you think a child is ultimately headed will determine what you teach, how you teach, and the culture of the school in which you teach. Does your school celebrate Feast days? Is chastity praised? Are the sacraments present? Do the boys learn chant? Do the girls ever meet real-live nuns? Can poor families get a discount? Is rap music ridiculed? Each of these questions will be answered, in the end, with reference to education's purpose. There is no escape. To ignore philosophy is merely to do it badly.

So what should the child become? Aristotle famously observed that all our actions aim at happiness.[33] This applies equally to our thinking about sex and war and economics as to learning. Happiness is the one thing which we cannot will for the sake of anything else. All recognize this. Where disagreement lies is not in the notion that education ought to promote students' well-being. Disagreement begins over what being "well" means. How might a reasonable person answer this question?

Options abound. Throughout the ages, some have said wealth, others honor, still others virtue. The Catholic view is based both on reason and revelation. Thomas Aquinas, the Church's greatest thinker, named happiness the "vision of the Divine Essence."[34] In this view happiness is a kind of action. Happiness is our *participation* in the divine life. It is that by which we come "to know, to love, and to serve [God], and so come to paradise" (CCC 1721). In our culture we too readily identify happiness with pleasure and power. It is therefore understandable that the majority of teens venerate pop musicians and pro athletes. How can believers offer a reasoned alternative? Certainly, money and fame are worthy goods. But they are relative goods. Through drama, through music, sport, liturgy, and, yes, even debate, we need to convince our youth what a thousand experiments have already proved: the joy of wealth is like the heat of a corpse, real for a time but sure to fade. The heart calls out for infinity. For this reason, the Church proposes the saint as a model: equipped with virtues, ennobled by culture in this life, striving for happiness in the next life.

Indeed, between the classical and Christian accounts of the value of learning there is broad agreement. Plato, like Augustine and Erasmus, posited life with God as man's highest end. Moderns do not typically aspire so high. From the point of view of the history of education, the dramatic break came not in the turn from classical pagan to Christian culture, but from Christianity to the Enlightenment. It was during the 18th and 19th centuries that the aim of education turned from contemplation to politics, and from the pursuit of virtue to merely material satisfactions. These days, the loftiest ideal our secular moralizers seem to raise is the notion of the "citizen."

Such, at least, is how many of our leaders speak. Each year senior students elect valedictorians, and universities set before

> *"There can be no true education which is not wholly directed to man's last end."*—Pius XI, *The Education of the Redeemed Man* (2011), §7

graduates speakers meant to inspire. Recently, Ohio State University invited Barak Obama to address their 10,000 best and brightest. At one point in the speech, the president encouraged the new grads to face boldly the trials ahead, to advance in confidence in spite of danger. Why is hope warranted? As he explained, because "our problems are man-made, therefore, they can be solved by man. And man can be as big as he wants."[35]

Is that so? Political goals may be lofty. They may even be worth one's life. But surely they are penultimate. What the president offered students at Ohio State was a humanism without God. It is a humanism without humility; as it turns out, it is a humanism that is humiliating. When our vision of the transcendent purpose of life is dimmed, our goals for education likewise at once shrivel and fantastically balloon. Education becomes narrowly political. Teachers raise consciousness so as to produce engaged citizens, while schools, for their part, become enlisted in the never-completed project of "social transformation." Aspiration turns from eschatology to utopia.

In sum, to teach is to shape. It is to bring a boy or a girl from potency to act, from the possible to the real. And into what image ought the teacher to form the student? Perhaps the most commonly cited passage from Vatican Two is also its most suggestive: "In reality it is only in the mystery of the Word made flesh that the mystery of man truly becomes clear" (*Gaudium et spes*, 22). The good teacher sees Christ, which is to say, he sees God and a man, a spirit, though fully flesh. He sees the master into whose image every student can hope to conform.

To solve the problems of education one cannot look merely to technical solutions. Education is and always has been a battle between the gods, a battle over ends. Deny Christ, and you cannot but deny man. Deny Christ and you end up treating man either as a beast or as an angel, or as a "citizen" doomed to rise no higher than the City of Man. A child of God is reducible to none of these things. He is, as St. Thomas might have said, a composite being, endowed with will, enlightened by reason, created for virtue, for culture, and for everlasting happiness. With the ends in view, we are ready to consider the means.

*Saint Cecilia and an Angel,*
Orazio Gentileschi and Giovanni Lanfranco

# 4

## The Methods of the Teacher:
## Imitation before Invention

I recently met a friend for breakfast at the edge of the rough part of town. Staring at me on the wall of the diner was a poster evidently hung by a social worker. The caption read, "It takes a village." The image beside was of a young mother with child, framed by a string of titles: teacher, doctor, social worker, and so forth. At the bottom—if memory serves—came "spouse." The message was clear. But it's the wrong message. The children don't belong to "everybody"; they are the charge, primarily, of the two bodies that became one body and produced a "somebody." Like all work, education requires healthy conditions. We want paved roads. We hope for civil neighbors. We need safe streets. Though man relies upon others to attain his end, there is an order to be followed: the state has its place, but it is at the back of the line.

The good news is ever new. And yet, to teach the Gospel in our day requires not only that we share our faith, but also that we identify the errors that seek to undermine Christian culture. Here I will mention two that belong to the practice of progressive teaching: that it takes a village to raise a child, and that children are naturally whole. The first is a mistake proposed by Hillary Clinton; the second by Jean-Jacques Rousseau (1712–1778), made familiar by his disciple and the father of progressive education, John

Dewey (1859–1952). In considering the methods of the teacher, I wish to consider first the limits to his authority, and then how a good teacher, one who sees himself working within the broad tradition of Catholic liberal learning, will encourage the imitation of masters before the mere expression of the self.

Consider a village. It is an attractive metaphor. It evokes images of children and parents, neighbors and elders working in concert. It is true that none of us are raised in a desert; a wilderness, perhaps. But every child, like every sapling, rises out from a native soul. Man is social. He cannot achieve his good without others. The question that divides social conservatives from progressives is not whether we need elders. The question that divides is: Who is the elder? Who among the villagers has the first right to comfort and to console, to chide and to correct? Historically, the family was acknowledged as the first educator of the child, with the state acting as a reverential ally.

The wisdom of this view is no longer everywhere appreciated. We are growing accustomed, perhaps like frogs in warming water, to seeing education as an instrument for political ends, and the teacher as a servant of the state. Our habit is of recent origin. Prior to the French Revolution, it was accepted that children were first in the trust of God, then of the parents and family, then the Church, and only in last position the state.

Our history is instructive. Throughout the 19th century, as the state began to replace the Church as the highest moral authority, so too did more areas of culture fall under the control of state-regulated bureaucracies. In France, for one, Napoleon closed all theological academies, including the ancient and prestigious Sorbonne.[36] In the 1870's, at the height of Bismarck's *Kulturkampf* (cultural struggle) against the Church, one out of two Prussian bishops was imprisoned or exiled—largely because of their defence of the Church's interest in education.[37]

In response to the rise of totalitarian regimes, the Church began to formalize what has become known as her Social Teaching. This teaching gives direction generally to the organization of political life, and particularly to education. It was Pope Leo XIII's *Rerum Novarum* (1891) which first articulated the principle of subsidiarity. The basic notion is simple: Mind your own business first so that you can keep your business first in mind. In other words, a "community of a higher order should not interfere" unduly in more basic communities (CCC 1883). Each man is to make his own bed. Each family is to raise its own children. We should not be mistaken; Leo did not call for libertarianism. The doctrine does nothing to weaken the demands of social justice. Indeed, its merit is best appreciated against the rise of militantly secular states. Far from cutting us off from our brother, subsidiarity is a call to each man to enter the community *as a genuine participant*. Each man is to be an agent, no man a tool. Applied to education, respect for subsidiarity safeguards the rightful autonomy of parents-as-educators, who, the *Catechism* says, bear "the first responsibility" (CCC 2223).

> "The teaching of the Church has elaborated the principle of subsidiarity according to which 'a community of a higher order should not interfere in the internal life of a community of a lower order. . . .'"—(CCC 1883)

This struggle over the identity of the elder only intensified during the 20th century. Thus, Hitler promoted his political vision through the Hitler Youth Camps, as did Lenin (and his wife) through the Young Pioneer Organization. After the fall of the Berlin wall, I studied for a short time in Eastern Europe, and taught in a formerly Communist school. What amazed me about the stories I heard was how consistently the Soviets preached their cause. Take my friend Mindaugas. The state provided his daycare. His school hosted a Communist club. During the summer he attended "pioneer camp"—kind of like Bible camp with a Communist twist. What the Soviets demanded, in short, was a total immersion in party doctrine.

So much for Europe. Until recent times North America had retained a closer link to both the English common law and the Catholic natural law traditions. We were spared many of the horrors of the 20th century in part because our piety placed a limit on our politics. Prior to the Republic, the man belongs to the sturdier polity of the Home. Thomas Jefferson once quipped, "Light and liberty go together."[38] There is truth to this sentiment. Democracy does depend upon educated citizens. Citizens need education, though, for much more than democracy. That power with the first and most abiding interest in the education of the child is not his state, nor his party, but his parents. In the familiar legal phrase, teachers act *in loco parentis*. Both our political tradition and our faith confirm that the teacher is first the servant not of the government, or even the Church, but of the family.

This view is old but not antiquated. From past and present debates illustrations could be multiplied. During the founding phase of Canada's democracy, for instance,

Canadians were conscious that the French Revolution had established a new *modus operandi* between citizen and state. Hence, in Russia, the Czar wanted education to reproduce monarchists; in Prussia, it aimed at fashioning militarists; in France, secular democrats. Heated discussion over the European template ensued and, in the end, Canadians rejected this foreign model. For instance, during a key 1858 parliamentary debate D'Arcy McGee, a fiercely Irish and Catholic Member of the House of Commons, argued successfully for the priority of the parents:

> The parent, not the political power, places the child in charge of the teacher; the teacher has his brief from the father or mother; they enter as avowed partners, with a mutual understanding, into the work of education; and the natural law, which prescribes the parent's duty, is not abrogated under such a partnership as that.[39]

The founding fathers of the American republic took a similar view. John Adams served as the second president of the United States (1797–1801), and before that had served two terms as vice-president under Washington. A lawyer turned diplomat and then politician, he and his wife Abigail enjoyed 54 years of happy marriage. Reflecting on the prospects of the new republic, and on the failure of past republics, he observed:

> The foundations of national morality must be laid in private families. In vain are schools, academies, and universities, instituted, if loose principles and licentious habits are impressed upon children in their earliest years. The mothers are the earliest and most important instructors of youth.

Good government depends upon good parents; and not only on good parents, but also on loving *spouses*. The stability of the home is the key to the flourishing of the people. And that stability is only maintained, in Adams' view, by an exclusive, faithful, permanent love between a husband and his wife. As Adams continued, "The vices and examples of the parents cannot be concealed from the children." If children are to be faithful, or gain the "just sense of the sacred obligations of morality or religion," they will have to see these qualities modeled by mom and dad.[40] In short, neither a strong economy, nor effective arms, nor caring laws, nor able teachers, can replace the moral authority of parents.

In our own time, defenders of this vision are still to be found. A prominent American senator, for instance, recently restated the natural-law argument for the priority of the family:

> Education begins and ends in the family. It begins in the family because the raising of children is first and foremost the duty and the right of parents, and because from the earliest stages of life children are picking up the habits and attitudes of their parents in how they approach the world.[41]

And of course Catholics can look to the *Catechism*. According to the Church, once parents bear a child, the duty to educate is inscribed into their DNA. Baring mental incapacity, no one can steal it away. And what are we to do with this right? As the *Catechism* states:

> As those first responsible for the education of their children, parents have the right *to choose a school for them* which corresponds to their own convictions. This right is fundamental. As far as possible parents have the duty of choosing schools that will best help them in their task as Christian educators. Public authorities have the duty of

guaranteeing this parental right and of ensuring the concrete conditions for its exercise. (CCC 2229)

Faith and political prudence point to similar conclusions. Parents: it is your duty to intervene. If your child's education is damaging them, fix it. If the culture of the classroom does not support the faith, change it. That might mean volunteering over recess; that might mean taking over a board of trustees; that might mean sending your girl to another district, or keeping your boy home. Whatever the case, according to God, you must maintain control and see to it that your child's education unfolds according to your wishes. The job of everyone else—politicians, principals, pastors, teachers, even taxpayers—is to help you make this happen.

So much for the village. Rousseau, it seems, would have us return to the jungle. If the first mistake about pedagogy concerns the identity of the teacher, the next concerns the nature of the *student*.

What a wonder is man, indeed! Up until the 18th century European civilization looked at men and women through the lens of Christ. For the righteous and wicked alike, death, judgment, heaven, and hell framed the border of a common image of man: divine in his origin, tarnished in his fall, glorious in his resurrection. Christian educators debated the details but not the ends; man they held in common. Not so today. The terms of disagreement changed with the Enlightenment, most forcibly with the publication of Rousseau's educational manifesto, *Emile* (1762).

From the point of view of faith, Rousseau's counsel leads to a ruined life. Many of Rousseau's observations on teaching methods are sound. But they are only accidentally so. He bases his philosophy of education, as he tells us, on a novel view of freedom—that children are born without any stain from sin. According to Rousseau, no longer is the battle of the moral life a combat between virtue and vice, excellence and decay. The true conflict is between authenticity and inauthenticity, between being other-directed and being inner-directed. The only lesson the child needs to learn is how he might be true to his natural self. Rousseau sets out the premise of his theory in the following terms:

> The truly free man wants only what he can do and does what he pleases. That is my fundamental maxim. It need only be applied to childhood for all the rules of education to flow from it.[42]

Man is born whole. It is society which corrupts. Man is born happy. It is hierarchy that frustrates. Sound familiar? In its day Rousseau's work caused a sensation. The French government confiscated the book; the Calvinist governors of Geneva burned it. Catholics everywhere predicted disaster. What we find in Rousseau is an early articulation of the view of *freedom as expression.*

Reasoned replies were also forthcoming. One year after its publication, the Italian priest-philosopher H.S. Gerdil (1718–1802) published *Reflections on the Theory and Practice of Education Against the Principles of Rousseau* (1763). In this detailed refutation, Fr. Gerdil showed how Rousseau's false anthropology led to his false pedagogy. Rousseau's theory can be reconciled neither with sound philosophy nor with Christian faith. Fr. Gerdil helpfully summarized Rousseau's five core principles:[43]

1. That prior to society man is self-sufficient and happy;

2. That we were born to be free adults, but laws and society plunge us back into dependent infancy;

3. That dependency upon others is repugnant to nature and the source of all evils for man;

4. That it is impossible to educate a man to have regard for himself and for others;

5. That a father has no right to command his children in that which is not ordered solely to their own good.

Rousseau's revolutionary achievement was to establish a new context for debates on pedagogy. Gone was the familiar story running from Adam to Christ. In its place was Emile, a child of Eden. Men and women might still seek a return to the blessed garden. They would find it, however, not through faith and the sacraments, but through a return to "authenticity." If Rousseau were head of your Board of Trustees, he'd appoint Jane Fonda as your principal.

Rousseau awakened in men a religious devotion to the self. It merely took secular educational theory two hundred years to fill in the details. Our mistrust of authority, our lack of dress codes, our patience for sloth, our fidelity to "child-centered" classrooms, our talk of values clarification can, in large measure, sooner or later, be laid at the feet of Rousseau's disciples in the social sciences, and to John Dewey.

Even in his own life Dewey's influence over education in the English-speaking world was enormous. Near the end of his career, he had both the privilege to see the growth of "progressive schools" and the opportunity to reflect upon their foundations. In words that echo Rousseau, John Dewey in 1938 stated the fundamental principles of the "new" education in contrast to the "old":

> To imposition from above is opposed expression and cultivation of individuality; to external discipline is opposed free activity; to learning from texts and teachers, learning through experience; to acquisition of isolated skills and techniques by drill, is opposed acquisition of them as means of attaining ends which make direct vital appeal; to preparation for a more or less remote future is opposed making the most of opportunities of present life; to static aims and materials is opposed acquaintance with a changing world.[44]

Dewey's caricature of 2,500 years of Western education is, of course, a straw man. What teacher would wish for "techniques by drill" that make no "vital appeal"? Who would hope to lock their daughter away from the "changing world"? Must preparation for the "remote future" (read: going to heaven) mean neglect of "present life" (read: getting a job)? Dewey himself, apparently, was a man of some culture. But, like most revolutionaries, he never had to sleep in the bed he made—or teach the sorts of students which progressive education was bound to produce. Dewey belonged to that generation of high-minded American liberals who married metaphysical skepticism to political

> *"What a piece of work is a man, how noble in reason, how infinite in faculties, in form and moving, how express and admirable in action, how like an angel in apprehension, how like a god!"*—Shakespeare, *Hamlet*, II.ii.1.302–7

optimism. Somehow, despite the death of God, despite the abyss, science and democracy would make everything turn out alright. Dewey praises "individuality" and "free activity" but cannot answer what is the good end of the individual or his free activity.[45]

The inconsistency of this approach took time to appreciate. Consider Dewey's achievement. With his left hand, Dewey stole from us the foundations for objective morality. All aims are in flux. All standards are self-generated. At the same time, he substituted with his right hand a new morality of "progress" in every way as "absolute" and inflexible as the one he sought to discard. A society that encourages mere freedom of expression is a society that soon finds itself crowded with the army of counselors, social service agents, and police officers needed to manage and contain the young people it has set adrift without rudder.

Some may object: Dewey's critique of traditional education may be flawed, but need we return to the 1950's school room? That is a fair question. Well, I don't recommend the tacky tiles, but what held up the old floor boards, in my view, remains sturdy. The tradition of Catholic education is living and dynamic. This means that the methods, the settings, and to some extent the curricula of Catholic schools can rightly vary over time and place. The foundation of the school, however, the moral vision that sustains the enterprise, cannot vary. The drama of heaven and hell, the virtues, the sacraments, the dignity of the person, the moral and mental disciplines implied by faith, all remain constants upon which the Catholic school must build and draw inspiration.

No doubt, in our time we've grown used to celebrating the colorful tapestry of America's "diversity." It is right to celebrate many kinds of diversity. All children are God's children. Every race and family of people belongs at the banquet of God's table. Still, the language of diversity too often shields a habit of moral indifference. In the context of the school, any talk of the language of objective good and evil can taste bitter to the tongue, and even appear inappropriate. But it need not. Indeed, nothing can be sweeter than the medicine of mercy mixed with a spoonful of truth. Truth makes us happy; mercy makes justice bearable. These are basic lessons every child needs to learn. Consider the consequences of the subjective vision of flourishing that's replaced the old.

A conversation comes to mind. Not long ago I was speaking with a young woman, "Lisa." She had graduated from a progressive high school where soft relativism reigned. Her parents divorced when she was young. She was struggling with drugs. Her boyfriend was a gangster. She believed in self-esteem. When we spoke she'd been in and out of rehab and, thankfully, had begun to set herself to better tasks. Her will was healing, which was wonderful. It was only her ideas that remained corrupt. During our conversation about the direction of her life, I asked questions about some of the articles of faith that her counselors had been pushing. The counselors promoted a "value-free" version of Rousseau. "Happiness is following your own path," they told her. Though she was doing better, she was concerned for her boyfriend. So I put to her this question: "If values are relative, what's wrong with being a gangster? I don't mean, 'tell me what might happen if you get caught.' What's wrong with the life of crime, if you decide this seems best for you?" Lisa thought for a moment. Then she said, "Yes, I've always wondered about that. What could I say?"

*interesting*

## The Methods of the Teacher: Imitation before Invention

On Rousseau's terms, on Dewey's terms, there is no good reply. In a childhood without moral clues, the self can only fall back upon itself; in a world where life is nothing but a journey, it really does not matter what you set for a destination, guns or no guns. Or, as the "Misfit" of Flannery O'Connor's short story puts it, "it's nothing for you to do but enjoy the few minutes you got left the best way you can. . . ."[46] Along this line of thinking, it is the child who knows best, not the teacher. Too many of us are roaming in the jungle with Rousseau. It would be better to return to our senses. *WOW.*

As those who have served in education know, our schools are filled with young men and women like Lisa. Our schools are overflowing with girls and boys looking for teachers who will set before them a model of a virtuous woman or man. Plainly, you cannot judge relative positions (of better or worse) without some sense of *best*, just as you can't call one line crooked until you have seen one that is straight. A similar rule applies to questions of pedagogy. Questions of method presume answers about ends. In order to judge which methods are correct, which pedagogical techniques are helpful, you will need to have in sight the measure, or the ends that you wish to pursue.

In answering this question, Christian educators have a considerable advantage. In the Christian view, custom, nature, reason, law, and revelation each can impart to the good teacher insight into what constitutes genuine flourishing. For the Christian teacher, then, the battle waged in every soul is a combat not between authenticity and inauthenticity. It is a battle between good and evil. The conflict in every soul is a conflict not between inner-directed and outer-directed behavior. It is a conflict between virtue and

YES ↓

vice. Virtue is the perfection of a power seeking its natural end. Vice, its decay. Effort over time produces an excellent habit. Power for good strengthens with practice. The boy who, little by little, shuffles to the edge of the diving board may, over time, conquer his dread of heights. The one who never tries is already conquered. In the old language that is what it means to be a coward. Virtue expands the will, vice turns you into a Gollum. When it comes to his or her education—contra Dewey—no child deserves to be stranded in the jungle, or the swamp.

I have argued that Rousseau's image of natural man is unnatural. Children are born to imitate: the question is not whether but *what*. I should like next to suggest a corollary. If we accept the Biblical and classical view of the human person, a primary task of teachers, it seems to me, is to set before children examples of excellence prior to encouraging their own creative expression. As a child matures, teachers add principles that support their students' practice. What implications does this view of man have for pedagogy?

Foremost it means that before one turns to invention, one should master *imitation*. I offer two illustrations of how this can work in practice. Both being teachers, my wife and I enjoy digging up old readers to see how our grandparents and great-grandparents would have been taught. The old readers almost always compare favorably to the new. What also amazes is how little the educational "methods" changed over time. Renaissance and Victorian manuals were not that unlike the practice of British, Canadian, and American schools prior to 1960.

## The Methods of the Teacher: Imitation before Invention

For my first exhibit, I take the most successful catechetical program produced in America. I refer, of course, to the *Baltimore Catechism*. As an instrument for religious education, it transmitted to generations the basic truths of religion. Though most parishes dropped it for coloring books in the 1970's, it's been making a return. Its method was simple. Through a question-answer format children learned to imitate a dialogue between disciple and master.

Question 870:

What is the Holy Eucharist?

Answer:

The Holy Eucharist is the Sacrament which contains the body and blood, soul and divinity, of our Lord Jesus Christ under the appearance of bread and wine.

Question 885:

What do you mean by the appearances of bread and wine?

Answer:

This change of the bread and wine into the body and blood of our Lord is called Transubstantiation.

Critics say that repetition is boring. Sometimes. When you consider that some 45% of Catholics do not know that the Church teaches the real presence (let alone believe it), a little more rote learning alongside *Veggie Tales* videos might not be a bad idea.[47] At least it would offer youth something to reject when they grow older, should they turn away. Unfortunately, too many of us don't even give our kids the option. Too many of our children reject a faith they never knew.

The method of imitation is by no means limited to rote learning. To get a sense of how traditional pedagogy encouraged imitation through a range of applications consider, next, the *Ratio Studiorum* (*The Order for Studies*). If the *Baltimore Catechism* was the most widely used religious-education text in North America, the *Ratio* set the standard for education in the liberal arts. Published in 1599, the "Order of Studies" incorporated the best of the scholastic and renaissance humanistic traditions of education. Its principles were disseminated through the hundreds of Jesuit colleges and universities that used them, including those across North America. It set standards that have, arguably, never been surpassed. To give you a taste of its methods, here is a generous selection of advice aimed at high-school literature teachers:

> [H]ave the members themselves deliver speeches or recite poems or give declamations, either from memory or ex tempore. With his approval, they may stage mock trials. [Teachers] may deliver a lecture and answer questions on it proposed by two or more of the members. Again they may defend theses and offer objections to them in an oratorical rather than a dialectical style.
>
> They may compose symbols or mottoes or again epigrams or brief descriptions. They may compose and solve riddles, or have a drill in invention, each one either on the spur of the moment or after reflection suggesting sources of arguments on a proposed topic. Or as practice in style they may suit metaphors or sentence patterns to a suggested argument. They may write out the plot of dialogues or tragedies, or the plan of a poem. They may

imitate a whole speech or poem of a famous orator or poet.

They may propose a symbol of some sort and have each member contribute to its meaning. They may assign the various books of some author and have each member of the academy make a selection of thoughts and expressions from the book assigned to him. Finally, let them cultivate the gift of eloquent expression and whatever is associated with its practice.[48]

Doesn't this make you want to be sixteen again? No doubt it was a simpler education. Perhaps, some might say, suited for a simpler age. No computers. No cooking class. No "anti-bullying" clubs. In the *Ratio*, every exercise aimed at elevating the culture of the mind. Memorization, drills, and repetitious exercises formed for centuries the backbone of early mental training. In advanced classes, the reading and imitation of classic authors made for the acquisition of style.

> "The bored 'graduates' of elementary and high schools . . . lack an object in life, they are unaware of the joy of achievement. They have been allowed to assume that happiness is a goal, rather than a by-product."—Hilda Neatby, *So Little for the Mind*, (1953), 11

"Creativity" receives little emphasis in a traditional scientific or literary formation, at least at first. This is not because the traditional educator is a slave to the past. It is because he knows that any worthwhile innovation will grow out of previous achievement. As Isaac Newton wrote, if he had seen "a little further" it was only "by standing on the shoulders of giants."[49] Like Augustine, like Shakespeare, Palladio, Rembrandt, Pascal, Mozart, Dickens, Turner, Tolkien, and others, the great scientist saw further because he first saw himself truly; that is, he recognized himself as a servant of truth and as an apprentice in a long tradition of learners.

The methods of education, in this view, aim not at self-expression. They reach much higher. They work toward the *expansion of freedom*. The will bent merely on its own appetite is as futile as the mind that insists that 3 plus 3 equals 7. Human freedom entails that you may remain stubborn if you wish; but nature has her own methods of correction. In mathematics, it is an empty account; in aesthetics; an ugly canvass; in morality, a ruined life.

In 1953 the most widely borrowed book at the Toronto public library was an essay from a woman raised on a farm in the grasslands of the Canadian prairie, in Saskatchewan. Hilda Neatby is not exactly a household name any longer. For a brief moment she was. A single woman, a Christian, and a historian by trade, she saw the effects of the "new" approach to teaching even before it had taken hold of the profession. *So Little for the Mind* predicted, well enough, that standards would fall.[50] More distressing, as Neatby saw, was the way that the new education drained from the young their zeal for life. Without a goal for his freedom, without a regiment to follow, a child will be thrown back upon his own resources. Yet this is precisely what children lack: developed resources. Apart from the wisdom of the elder, they will tend to grasp whatever happiness is at hand, and their time will be lost to trivialities. At fourteen, who wants to crack open the algebra when you could plug in *Grand Theft Auto V*?

Against the errors of our age we might retrieve two noble contributions from the past. First: that it is the parent, not the state, nor the professional, who is the first teacher and last authority. Second: that the child is good though damaged; that he learns first through imitation; and that progress in culture proceeds best when he can imitate the finest of others before he is asked to invent for himself.

*Geometria*, Hieronymous Cock

Goals

# 5

# The Matter of Learning:
# The Sprightly Seven Arts

If the ends of a Catholic education are the acquisition of heavenly happiness (final goal), formation in a vibrant moral and intellectual culture (proximate goal), and useful skills (immediate goal), of what should the liberal arts curriculum consist?

The word *school* comes from the Greek *schole,* which means leisure. Schools are houses of leisure. Inside their temple walls the young are freed for serious play. Capitalists tend to view wealth-generation as man's highest activity. They produce schools that look and function like factories. Not so a Catholic school. *Ora et labora:* Pray and work. From St. Benedict onward, Christians have demonstrated how a love for the next life can humanize and divinize the activities of this life. Like a church, the very dimensions of a Catholic school, the art and iconography that adorn its walls, the spirit of devotion to Our Lady, are to announce its sacred character. As from the *Congregation for Catholic Education*:

> From the first moment that a student sets foot in a Catholic school, he or she ought to have the impression of entering a new environment, one illumined by the light of faith, and having its own unique characteristics.[51]

And what of the books? Needless to say, the music, sport, and liturgy of a Catholic school will exert a greater force on

69

the young than the words they read, though these too count. In a good school, students and faculty become excellent at learning, each according to their proper age. Each has its own trial and reward. What suits a man would crush a boy.

> And one man in his time plays many parts
> His acts being seven ages.[52]

Hence, for every age, there is a school:

The age of infancy: 0 to 7 in the school of play;
The age of the schoolboy: 7 to 15 in the school of nature;
The age of the lover: 15 to 25 in the school of literature;
The age of the soldier: 25 to 45 in the school of experience;
The age of the governor: 45 to 65 in the school of suffering;
The age of the counselor: 65 till senility in the school of death;
The age of second infancy: in the school of dreams.[53]

Our focus is on the schoolboy and the lover, though I wish to reflect on them from the view of a college professor. The encounter between student and teacher is like a dance. In the classroom the text is the music. The music sets the tempo. However bright the melody, if you arrive with club feet, the dance will decay into a shuffle. Most students come to college with club feet. This is not because they are dull. Fed on dreary, mass-produced, politically-monitored textbooks, their brains have merely been starved for oxygen.

It's not that the parents or teachers are mean. It's that the kids have suffered under a dictatorship of relativism. Johnny can't tell right from wrong because Johnny's parents don't know themselves. And so, their passions malformed, their music coarse, they arrive at university as slaves. Too many are addicted to iPhones and Facebook: that is, they are addicted to themselves and to fashion. Money is not the problem, nor is leisure. 15–24 year olds spend a mere 7–10 minutes a day on voluntary reading versus 2–2.5 hours in front of a television.[54] The problem is they were never taught to enjoy their leisure when they were kids and so, now that they are old enough, Plato, St. Thomas, and Shakespeare appear hard and hardly worth the effort.

> *"From the first moment that a student sets foot in a Catholic school, he or she ought to have the impression of entering a new environment. . . ."*— Congregation for Catholic Education, *The Religious Dimensions of a Catholic School, §25*

What's the remedy? Not much can be done by the time a student has reached college. It's in the middle schools and high schools that the battle for Catholic education needs to be fought and won. At 13 a young girl or boy does not need Aristotle. What they should have in childhood are nursery rhymes, drawing lessons, vigorous games, practice working with animals and gardens, silly poetry, Beatrix Potter, Robin Hood, and later, Robert Louis Stevenson, L. M. Montgomery, the Bible, and Plutarch.

The goal of the early curriculum is to stiffen their muscles and fill their minds with images of beauty. By 15 they are ready to begin thinking about them. In elementary school, children learn by imitation and repetition. In high school, they learn through argument and sweat. They need to take risks; they want desperately to think about the permanent questions—this is usually best done indirectly through stories, not rigorous dialectic. Greek tragedies, Dickens, Austin, Tolkien and the rest will paint in vivid color the landscape of adult life into which they will soon step.

Feed them on textbooks and their natural appetite for wonder will be lost. Why read about the "Middle Ages" when you could have Chaucer lead you on a pilgrimage? Why be preached at about "Social Justice" when you could read 1st and 2nd *Samuel* or *A Tale of Two Cities*? Before you lead children to gather the harvest of the Great Books, what they need—to borrow a phrase from John Senior—is the thousand *Good Books*, which will strengthen their native hunger for noble beauty. Only a mind filled with examples of heroes and villains, of angels and devils, of battles and romances, will be able at 17 to begin the more laborious work of thinking rationally about war, God, and sex. The work of a liberal curriculum is to prepare the soil. Don't let it blow away.

The first task of a liberal education is to train the mind to think. What does that entail? At the least, to think well is to understand connections between causes and effects; it is to acquire skills that allow you to read, write, count, and speak with intelligence. It is to grasp how differing methods (scientific, mathematical, rhetorical) correspond to and are derived from the differing objects we encounter in nature and culture (matter, number, politics); it is, in short, to attain what Cardinal Newman termed the "enlargement of mind."[55] A tall order. Even if we cannot completely encompass its range, we may state its limit. To aim at intellectual virtue does not necessitate that one master every subject. It demands only knowledge of first principles in a few subjects. As Aristotle remarked, an educated man should be able to form "a fair off-hand judgment as to the goodness or badness of the method used" in any argument.[56] One fruit of intellectual virtue, then, is the ability to know when what has been offered is an opinion, when it

*Payoff*

has been proven, and the difference between these two.

We spoke earlier about the virtue of imitation. Though the technique still applies, by the time the child has turned adolescent emphasis must shift. Reason, not emotional intelligence, not life-skills, not self-esteem, is what liberal study aims to perfect at this stage. Sewing, baking, soccer . . . : each of these and more have their place within a child's formation; but the school that once loses sight of its first task, its guiding star, is likely never to find its way home. By mixing mental discipline with other, sometimes laudable goals, contemporary high-schools and colleges often lose their reason for existence. When schools make intellectual formation secondary, they not only become ineffective. They turn learning into a chore and leave much undone.

So, what is the *matter* of the curriculum? On what objects should the mind exercise itself? Until recently, the curriculum had been formed around the seven liberal arts: grammar, logic, rhetoric, arithmetic, geometry, astronomy, and music. I name these disciplines "sprightly" because they quicken, expand, stiffen, refine, and make flexible the mind; the arts, we might say, are the oxygen of the intellect. Here is my account of how the tradition settled upon these seven.

Signs exist for the sake of things. We point our finger toward the blue jay to signal our delight; we compose a sonnet to show our passion. As St. Augustine argued at the opening of his most important book on education, *On Christian Teaching*, teaching requires mastery of signs. Words are signs. The better you can use them, the better you can describe things both outside and inside your head. In the structure of the traditional liberal-arts curriculum the study of verbal signs constitutes the *trivium*. Grammar observes the order within thought; rhetoric observes the order within emotion; logic observes the order within the mind. Words are the first and most important tools by which we grasp the nature of things. They are not the only tools.

Next comes the *quadrivium*. In the order of the liberal curriculum these comprise the mathematical arts. While verbal signs allow us to signify the qualitative nature of things, numbers signify quantities. Hence arithmetic, geometry, astronomy, and music provide access to things insofar as they have extension and occupy space ("music" here refers to its theory as embedded in ratios). Writing in the 12$^{th}$ century, on the eve of the birth of Christendom's universities, Hugh of St. Victor praised the seven liberal arts in this way:

> For these, one might say, constitute the best instruments, the best rudiments, by which the way is prepared for the mind's complete knowledge of philosophic truth. Therefore they are called by the name trivium and quadrivium, because by them, as by certain ways (*viae*), a quick mind enters into the secret places of wisdom.[57]

Interested in finding a "common core" you can trust? Those parents and teachers wishing to reconstruct a basic curriculum for their children might consider the one that has served the West for the past twenty-five centuries. It's been field-tested, too, in the laboratories of Greece, under Plato; in Italy, under Benedict; in the medieval and Renaissance academies attended by Thomas Aquinas and Thomas More; in the Jesuit prep schools from India to Mexico; and even, until about 1975, by the boys and girls at your local St. Joseph's elementary in Boston, Philadelphia, St. Louis,

Houston, Los Angeles, or Vancouver. The trials have yielded near-universal results. The seven liberal arts are indispensable not because they teach us all we need to know. The arts are useful because they teach us how to learn; they serve not as the summit of wisdom, but as its gateways. The good teacher, then, will use a curriculum that trains students to read *signs*.

Reflect back on your youth. Recall the great and the regrettable you encountered in your classroom. Your good teachers served as windows. They opened up vistas not yet seen; bad teachers tended to block the view. Perhaps one fine professor taught literature, another physics, yet a third, piano. What unites these mentors? Evidently, it was not their subject matter. The unity, it seems to me, belongs at the level of form. Every helpful teacher grasps the connection between signs (words, numbers, notes) and things; they can point, and they can excite. Quite simply, to teach is to see, and to invite others to look for themselves. A good curriculum supports this ambition.

As both the history of education and those philosophers esteemed by the Church seem to suggest, the seven liberal arts are the best means for a student to learn how to make a beginning, to learn how to *learn*. Which books to read precisely, in what order precisely, and with what exercises precisely, are matters not of first principle but of prudential application. Those who would enjoy thinking further along these lines might begin with Dorothy Sayer's essay "The Lost Tools of Learning," then move on to Laura Berquist's *Designing Your Own Classical Education*, and perhaps to Jacques Maritain's *Education at the Crossroads*.[58] And so we proceed to our final question: after we get the books right, where do we turn next?

*Children of the Sea*, Josef Israëls

# 6

# The Coming Renewal: Faith in the Future

We return to our children. Children are like barometers. They tell you which way the atmosphere is moving. When asked how many babies they want to raise, today's teens' responses typically fall into one of three groups: 13% say they want none or one; predictably, 73% either say that they want two or three; and 14% say they want four, five, or more children.[59] Focus on that first group and on the last. These children represent the two possible futures for North American education. While the number of irreligious kids has increased, the identity of the religiously conservative kids has strengthened. The future is not all gloomy. Catholic education may be in crisis, but signs of renewal abound. We opened these essays by reflecting upon the crisis in education initiated some two generations ago. That past we cannot unmake. We conclude by looking toward the future, and to the hopeful signs of a coming Second Spring in Catholic education. Here are a few of them, starting from the top.

Among colleges, after the long winter of Catholic higher education in the 1980's and 1990's, Canada now boasts a few young, upstart colleges whose futures are not yet secured, but nonetheless give cause for hope. Some of the graduates belonging to the John Paul II generation have taken up teaching assignments themselves. Catholic Christian Outreach continues to thrive. Similar movements of reform are afoot elsewhere, as, for instance, in England, Ireland, Austria, and Australia.

In the United States, the scene is more dynamic. Since the 1970's, a young crop of colleges has been struggling to establish itself as an alternative to the mainstream institutions: among them, we could point to California's Thomas Aquinas College, New England's Thomas More College, Virginia's Christendom College, Ave Maria University in the South, or Benedictine or Steubenville in the Midwest. All of these colleges are annually highlighted in *The Newman Guide*. But university renewal has hardly been restricted to these. The leaven of Saint John Paul II's *Ex Corde Ecclesiae* has begun to work its way through the dough.[60] All over the U.S.—where the renewal of Catholic education is not outright denied—administrators and professors have engaged in an exercise of communal soul-searching. Among the two dozen or so Jesuit universities, opportunities for service internships abound. I say nothing of the dozens of chaplaincies, FOCUS groups, Newman Centers (like the one hosted by the Oratorians near the University of Pittsburgh) and specialized graduate programs like Denver's Augustine Institute. Today, an ambitious twenty-something can find intellectual fellowship in places like Villanova's Augustinian Institute, Princeton's Witherspoon Institute, the Center for Catholic Studies at St. Thomas University, or Notre Dame's Center for Ethics and Culture. Opportunities for formation are not what they used to be, but we've long left the dark decades.

Then there is the new generation of private and parochial

schools, both those newly founded and those newly celebrating their Catholic identity. Catholic charter schools are appearing like so many buds in April. Again, in Canada one could point to Our Lady of Grace School in Fredericton, New Brunswick. Our Lady of Grace was begun a few years back by a local pro-life doctor. The school, housed in the rented basement of a local Protestant church, is tiny and poor. It takes kids other schools don't want. Discipline is strict. Everyone learns Latin. Teachers walk their students through the riches of a classical curriculum. Imagine what they could do with a hundred-thousand-dollar donation? In Ontario, we could point to Wayside Academy. Archbishop Terrence Prendergast of Ottawa, noting that great things often come from small beginnings, has argued that Wayside is a sign of hope for a new springtime of Catholic education; he calls it "a centre of faith, a nucleus of culture, and a pole for the Christian community."[61] In the United States, examples abound. Many schools—like St. Francis of Assisi Elementary in the Diocese of New Hampshire—are attracting new students, in part because of a renewed sense of how the liturgy can set the rhythm of the school week; other schools—like Minnesota's Chesterton Academy—are finding inspiration in the richness of a classical curriculum.

Organizations and parent-led associations devoted to educational renewal are on the rise, too. Sophia Institute for Teachers, the Institute for Catholic Liberal Education, and the Cardinal Newman Society are among the new generation of "para-academic" groups strengthening our Catholic schools. Within a short drive from our home (in New England), parents can choose from some half-dozen classically oriented schools or cooperatives.

Which leads us, last but not least, to the homeschoolers. In the United States, an estimated 3–4% of the student population, or about two million children, are homeschooled.[62] These kids sit comfortably at the top of their class. Since the 1970's numerous researchers have compared educational outcomes of different systems of schooling. These studies consistently rank homeschooled kids between 15 and 30 percentage points above national averages. A recent national survey in the United States compared the educational achievement of 11,739 homeschooled children to national averages. Here's what was uncovered. Across disciplines, homeschooled kids excel: in reading they are at the 89th percentile; in math, at the 84th; and in science, at the 86th.[63] Research abroad confirms the same. Public education is healthier in Canada. And yet, in reading, for instance, a home-educated high-school student ranks 35 points (or at the 85th percentile) higher than the average student.[64] Never mind religion—82% of these young people are still involved in religious groups, compared to 13% of non-home-schooled Canadians—once they become adults they are more interesting. Compared to their peers, they are about four times more likely to attend a classical music performance, twice as likely to have voted in a federal election, far more likely to read a book, and earn more money.[65] Incidentally, whether or not a homeschooling parent has a teaching certificate or teaching degree makes almost no difference to their student's success.[66] I mention this not to argue that all students should be taught at home, but to

*Once we lost confidence in the world-transforming mission of the faith, it was only a matter of time till the schools should turn flabby.*

illustrate the indispensable role of parents—even parents who wouldn't normally see themselves as good "educators."

The recent history of Catholic education in North America has been, in large measure, the story of a glorious legacy ingloriously undermined. Once we lost confidence in the world-transforming mission of the faith, it was only a matter of time till the schools would turn flabby. An anecdote comes to mind. A friend of ours, a mother of five, recently took a tour of her local Catholic elementary school. Somewhere along the way she wanted to raise the question of Catholic devotions. What proportion of teachers practice their faith? How often do the children go to Mass? Will they study the lives of the saints? Another parent, who had the same questions, spoke first. "We're not Catholic," this woman began. "Will it be a problem if we send our kids here?" To which the guide reassured, "Oh no, you won't feel uncomfortable. We're not like that anymore."

Needless to say, our friend had her answer. I wonder: should just *anyone* feel at home in a Catholic school? By emptying our halls of statues; by forgetting to display our rosaries; by hiding from parents our holy hours, our confessions, our cassocks, our processions, all solemnly tucked away in some back-room utility closet, we removed from sight the treasures that made the school sacred, and the classrooms worth defending. As Benedict XVI told educators during his visit to America, "First and foremost every Catholic educational institution is a place to encounter the living God who in Jesus Christ reveals his transforming love and truth."[67] If the recent past provides any indication of future trends, only those schools willing to provide a place of genuine "encounter" are likely to attract the support and fidelity of Catholic parents and their children.

I conclude by painting a picture for you of two girls. The lives of these young people mirror the alternative futures for Catholic education within English-speaking countries. Let's call them Britne and Mary. Each belongs to one of the extreme demographic sets we've already discussed. Britne represents the harshly secular kids who don't want to grow up to be parents; Mary represents those who look forward to a big family, or might even consider joining a religious order. When she's a bit older, Britne will speak for the "lifestyle liberals." She and others like her come largely from permissive but socially respectable parents. Mom and Dad both worked, had their boy and girl, attended church at Easter and at funerals. Britne's parents bought a house in the suburbs; when she was 8 they took her and her kid brother Devon to Disneyland; when she was 12, Dad bought a new car and left Mom for a new wife. Britne's a survivor. She's learned to adapt. She doesn't hate her parents. In fact, living away from home every second week is not bad. Dad buys her things Mom can't afford, and on the weekends away she can stay out pretty much as late as she likes. In the eyes of most, she'll turn out to be a nice person.

Britne and the kids like her largely come from open concept families. The difference is she will have few of the social hang-ups that her baby-boomer parents had way back in the 1990's—or even in the early 2000's. When trying to account for how he could vote against gay marriage in 2001 and then spearhead the Canadian federal government's Bill C-38 and block a national referendum on the definition of marriage in 2005, Catholic Prime Minister

Paul Martin replied: "much has changed since that day."[68] When an American president unveiled his new-found preference for homosexual marriages his justification was equally laconic. His views, he said, had evolved. It was New York State's declaration against traditional marriage that carried his thinking forward. "That's part of the—the evolution that I went through," he observed in a 2012 interview. "I asked myself—right after that New York vote took place, if I had been a state senator, which I was for a time—how would I have voted? And I had to admit to myself, 'You know what? I think that—I would have voted yes.'"[69] Indeed, these days evolution happens even among Supreme Court Justices.[70]

Britne's views, like many of our political leaders', are fluid. She may be a conformist. But at least she is still polite. If you are handicapped, she won't park in your stall—though she will vote for euthanasia. If you're handicapped in the womb, she'll say it's only compassionate to terminate you. She's not much for religion. She recycles. When she turns 27, she'll tote her golden retriever in the back of her Subaru hatchback. Her parents voted for liberal politicians: she does or she doesn't. If she does, she's likely to vote for members of a Green Party.

Britne represents one possible future for North America's teens. But she's not the only girl on the block. The other future belongs to Mary—she's the one who wants kids, and goes to church. Mary belongs to a 15–20% demographic set that we might call the "rebellious conservatives." Some of these come from strong families. Others grew up in open concept homes like the "lifestyle liberals," but rebelled against the rebellion. They've suffered through their parents' own painful experimentations; maybe they've tried drugs. Whatever they've done, they've seen up-close the effects of moral anarchy, and pulled back in dismay. Most of these young adults are Catholics and Evangelicals. Some of them study in your classroom or around your kitchen table.

Why should we reclaim the principles of Catholic education? The most compelling answer is seen in the faces of these two girls. We might do well to consider their futures: Which do I want my daughter to step into—or my son to marry? As I have tried to document, the principles of progressive education, spawned by Rousseau, nurtured by John Dewey, and for the last several generations harvested in many of our classrooms, have precipitated a crisis in Catholic education; even more, they have left our students largely uncatechized and uninspired by the faith we profess. Our children deserve to gain more than the mere freedom of expression. They want desperately to learn the virtues that will offer the freedom of excellence. Such is the only freedom worthy of a child of God.

If I have been critical of our schools in these pages, it is because there is much to admire; and where we have pointed to weakness, it is because there is potential for greater strength. The lesson to draw is not that all kids need to be educated in the same way. The basic principles of Catholic education are few, their potential applications many. The first lesson, it seems to me, is simple. The primary responsibility, and hence the heaviest burden, falls upon us parents. If your child's education is broken, find allies, and fix it.

May we all—parents, teachers, politicians, and, yes, even

preachers—reclaim as our birthright the first principles of Catholic education, so that armed with philosophy, encouraged by faith, and sustained by hope, we may love well and form our children wisely.

# Appendix 1:
# Discussion Questions

## Review and Discussion Questions

### Chapter 1: The Crisis of Catholic Education

1. According to Dawson, what is the "crisis" of Western education?
2. Describe the "positivistic" view of reason. Why does Benedict XVI think it deficient?
3. What distinguishes liberal from servile education?
4. Money is necessary to sustain the enterprise of Catholic education. Why is it never sufficient?

### Chapter 2: The Schools and Our Children

1. John Paul II proposed that the "greatest contribution" that Catholic educators can make is to restore the conviction that human beings can "grasp the truth of things." Why is moral relativism more damaging to culture than, say, poverty or social inequality?
2. Identify three statistics cited here which you or, perhaps someone else, might find surprising. In what sense do these statistics surprise?
3. In your experience, what is helpful and what is harmful in the movement to encourage students' "self-esteem"?
4. Consider those teens you know who retain a vital faith. In your experience, is it the parish, the school, or the

family that seems most to encourage their Catholic identity? What role does each play?

## Chapter 3: The Purposes of Education

1. Distinguish between the three senses of the "end" of education.
2. Describe the two senses of "freedom" that serve as the basis for competing views of the purpose of education.
3. According to Aristotle, what ought a liberal education teach a child to do?
4. On what basis does the Church teach that parents are the first educators?

## Chapter 4: The Methods of the Teacher

1. Name three ways a Catholic teacher (at home or at school) could make his or her classroom feel more "Catholic."
2. What is true and what is false in the metaphor "it takes a village to raise a child"?
3. Identify two pedagogical methods that you have found useful in your own experience. Name one from the *Ratio Studiorum* that you might consider implementing.

## Chapter 5: The Matter of Learning

1. From your experience, describe the sorts of intellectual and moral changes that occur during the child's transition from "schoolboy" to "lover."
2. Work, it is often said, is for the sake of leisure. How can the right use of leisure support a child's study?

3. Describe, conceptually, the difference between the trivium and the quadrivium.
4. Why does Hugh of St. Victor praise the liberal arts? Why do some schools seem to ignore them?

## Chapter 6: The Coming Renewal

1. It was suggested that teens can be, broadly, lumped into one of three groups. Does this division resonate with your own experience?
2. Homeschooled students consistently outperform students in conventional classrooms. What helpful lessons about education might any teacher draw from this?
3. What are two practical steps you could take toward making your school or classroom more Catholic?
4. Imagine you are the principal of your school (or superintendant of your district). What structural changes might you propose that would encourage further renewal?

# Appendix 2:
## Guide to Further Study

## A. Magisterial Documents

Benedict XVI, "Address to Catholic Educators"

Delivered in Washington, DC in 2008, this is Benedict's synthesis of recent magisterial teaching on the role of education in the mission of the Church. Offering inspiration to anyone devoted to the renewal of Catholic colleges and schools, he memorably declared that "First and foremost every Catholic educational institution is a place to encounter the living God who in Jesus Christ reveals his transforming love and truth." The text is a fitting reply to the renegade 1967 "Land O'Lakes" declaration.

John Paul II, *Fides et Ratio* (Encyclical on Faith and Reason)

This is the most important intervention on the relation between philosophy and theology since Leo XIII's *Aeterni Patris* (1879). The pope argues that faith and reason are two wings which, together, allow the Christian to rise to God. The centrality of Thomas' teaching is reaffirmed. It exposes the causes of the crisis of faith, stating that "Nihilism is at the root of the widespread mentality which claims that a definitive commitment should no longer be made, because everything is fleeting and provisional" (§46). The document should be read alongside the encyclical *Splendor Veritatis* (on renewal in moral theology) and the constitution *Ex Corde Ecclesiae* (on the renewal of universities).

# The Case for Catholic Education

## John Paul II, *Ex Corde Ecclesiae* (Apostolic Constitution on Catholic Universities)

This document established objective norms for securing the Catholicity of Catholic universities worldwide. "Catholic teaching and discipline are to influence all university activities, while the freedom of conscience of each person is to be fully respected. Any official action or commitment of the University is to be in accord with its Catholic identity" (Art. 2 §4). The text, juridical in nature, has stiffened Catholic identity in most places, been derided in some places, but reignited conversation in all places.

## John Paul II, *Familiaris Consortio* (Apostolic Exhortation on the Role of the Family in the Modern World)

Building off of a century of Catholic social teaching, John Paul II here articulates a manifesto for the civilizing role of the family. "The ministry of evangelization carried out by Christian parents is original and irreplaceable" (§53). The message is simple: no family, no society; heal the family, heal the culture.

## Archbishop Michael Miller, CSB, *The Holy See's Teaching on Catholic Schools*

Originally delivered as a lecture while Miller was Secretary for the Vatican's Congregation for Education, it offers a concise statement of Catholic teaching on learning. In the light of the current decline of Catholic schools he unapologetically observes: "Ensuring their Catholic identity is the Church's greatest educational challenge." Miller names five marks of a genuinely Catholic school. He proposes that Catholic schools ought to undergo an accreditation process that offers "assurance of their Catholic identity."

Pontifical Council for the Family, *The Truth and Meaning of Human Sexuality: Guidelines for Education within the Family*

A helpful document published by this Pontifical Council on the principles and practice of chastity education. Attentive to the present "eclipse of the truth about man" (§1), it draws upon the best of developmental psychology. The text offers prudential guidelines and "best practices" for how to introduce children to the gift and mystery of human sexuality.

Second Vatican Council, *Gravissimus Educationis* (Declaration on Christian Education)

Vatican Two's twelve-paragraph statement on Christian education. A good point of departure for anyone wishing to begin to "think with the Church" on the dignity of learning, on the rights of parents, on the vocation of teachers, on the duties of pastors, and on the role of the state.

Leo XIII, *Rerum Novarum* (Encyclical on Capital and Labor)

Here lies the immediate origin of the Church's social teaching—not to be confused with some Catholics' teaching on "social justice." Leo's most important contribution to education is his definition and defense of the principle of subsidiarity. (See also the *Catechism* 1883–1885.)

## B. Philosophical and Cultural Studies

Aquinas, *On Disputed Questions* (Question 11)

Here Aquinas takes up the nature of knowledge and the role of the teacher. Study of this should be supplemented by his mature treatments in the *Summa*, as for example at I q.84 aa 5–6. Ralph McInerny's *A First Glance at St. Thomas*

*Aquinas: A Handbook for Peeping Thomists* (Notre Dame: University of Notre Dame Press, 1990) remains invaluable. Fr. Vivian Boland's *St. Thomas* (London: Bloomsbury Press, 2014) leads the reader further.

## Augustine, *On the Teacher, On Christian Doctrine, On Order* (De Ordine)

These represent Augustine's most important discussions on teaching and learning. On the question of knowledge, Augustine's *On the Teacher* picks up where Plato's *Meno* left off. *On Order* offers a Christianized vision of the liberal arts; *On Christian Doctrine* explains the place of Biblical interpretation. Orientation can be found in Ryan Topping, *St. Augustine* (London: Bloomsbury Press, 2014).

## Christopher Dawson, *Crisis of Education in the West* (Washington, DC: Catholic University of America Press, 2010)

Dawson is widely regarded as the finest Catholic historian of recent times. Like John Senior (see his *Restoration of Christian Culture*), Dawson saw that any return to the Great Books of our civilization would fail without a return to the habits of civility. The modern mind is homeless because it knows not whence it sprung. What is needed is a retrieval of our cultural memory. After a guided tour through the rise and decline of Western education, Dawson provocatively proposes "a reorientation of higher studies with the concept of Christian culture as the integrating factor—a new humanist studies oriented towards Christian culture rather than classical culture in the old style or the contemporary Western secular culture in the new style" (p. 118).

## Stratford Caldecott, *Beauty for Truth's Sake: On the Re-enchantment of Education* (Grand Rapids, MI: Brazos Press, 2009)

Caldecott calls for a re-enchantment of education which would train students to grasp the meaning and order inherent within creation. Conversant with the theory of the classical liberal arts, and following upon the work of Benedict XVI, among others, he shows how all education finds its fulfillment in the liturgy. This work is complemented by his more recent *Beauty in the Word: Rethinking the Foundations of Education* (Tacoma, WA: Angelico Press, 2012).

Peter Kreeft, *Socratic Logic: A Logic Text Using Socratic Method, Platonic Questions, and Aristotelian Principles*, ed. 3.1 (Notre Dame, IN: St. Augustine's Press, 2010)

You may want this before you send your students to the *Posterior Analytics.* A marvelous text that introduces students and teachers not only to the fundamentals of logic but also to the joys of identifying fallacies, structuring essays, and mastering Aristotle's 10 categories.

C. S. Lewis, *The Abolition of Man* (London: Harper Collins, 1974)

Progressive education produces men without chests. In this work, Lewis explains why. "In a sort of ghastly simplicity we remove the organ and demand the function. We make men without chests and expect of them virtue and enterprise. We laugh at honour and are shocked to find traitors in our midst. We castrate and bid the geldings be fruitful" (p. 26).

Curtis L. Hancock, *Recovering a Catholic Philosophy of Elementary Education* (Mount Pocono, PA: Newman House Press, 2005)

An excellent discussion of what is at stake, philosophically, in the battles over education. Parents and teachers will find his final section—a series of short questions and answers—especially helpful.

Michael D. O'Brien, *A Landscape with Dragons: The Battle for Your Child's Mind* (San Francisco, CA: Ignatius Press, 1998)

"The undermining of a child's perceptions in forms that are apparently harmless may be the most destructive [attack] of all" (p. 73). Parents and teachers will find few better guides to literature than O'Brien. This work shows how a shift in philosophy wreaks havoc on culture, particularly on the literature for the young.

Anthony Esolen, 10 *Ways to Destroy the Imagination of Your Child* (Wilmington, DE: ISI Books, 2010)

If you like *The Screwtape Letters*, you'll enjoy this.

## C. Histories of Education

Histories of education range from uneven to awful. In the 20th century, "education" as a discipline broke away from philosophy and theology and was picked up by psychologists. Governed by the guiding lights of experimental psychology (like Dewey) or post-Marxist philosophy (like Nel Noddings), contemporary historians of the "philosophy of education" tend alternately to ignore or deplore the influence of Christianity. There are exceptions. For ancient and early Christian education Henri Marrou's *History of Education in Antiquity* has not been surpassed. Reliable general surveys can be found in James Bowen's three-volume *History of Education* as well as J.J. Chambliss' *Philosophy of Education: An Encyclopedia*. Beyond these, one does best to turn to specialized studies (e.g., on Augustine, Thomas, Erasmus, Newman), or to the sources themselves.

## D. Journals

*Catholic Education: A Journal of Inquiry and Practice* provides access to some of the best peer-reviewed research on Catholic education today. The journal is generous in its interests and broad in its orientation—including, for instance, both philosophical and statistically based research. Also of note is *International Studies in Catholic Education, The International Journal of Christianity and Education,* and *Studies in Catholic Higher Education* of the Cardinal Newman Center. *Logos: A Journal of Catholic Culture,* published by St. Thomas University's Center for Catholic Studies, publishes excellent articles on Catholic culture of interest to educators.

## E. Sociological Studies

Two outstanding sociologists of religion in North America are Christian Smith and Reginald Bibby. Bibby's work focuses on Canada, Smith's on the United States. Among titles useful for grasping the dynamics of teen culture are Bibby's *The Emerging Millennials: How Canada's Newest Generation is Responding to Change and Choice* (Lethbridge, AB: Project Canada Books, 2009), and Smith's *Souls in Transition: The Religious and Spiritual Lives of Emerging Adults* (Oxford: Oxford University Press, 2009). For recent and forthcoming research see these authors' websites.

## F. Homeschooling

Kimberly Hahn and Mary Hasson, *Catholic Education: Homeward Bound* (San Francisco: Ignatius Press, 1996)

Two veteran moms and educators, well versed in the Catholic vision for the family, offer an encouraging guide for parents considering homeschooling.

Laura Berquist, *Designing Your Own Classical Curriculum: A Guide to Catholic Home Education* (San Francisco, CA: Ignatius Press, 1998)

A marvelously practical guide by a graduate of Thomas Aquinas College and mother of six. Alongside her apology for Classical education is included well-organized booklists useful for teachers or parents wishing to form students in the traditional liberal arts.

Susan Wise Bauer and Jessie Wise, *The Well-Trained Mind: A Guide to Classical Education at Home* (New York: W.W. Norton & Company, 2009)

A good complement to Berquist's work; while more detailed, for that reason perhaps it is more cumbersome.

## G. Websites

Cardus Religious Schools Initiative [www.crsi.nd.edu]

Do religious schools promote civic engagement? Are children at Catholic or public schools more likely to go to college? When do homeschooled children marry? This site, hosted by the University of Notre Dame, posts scholarly research of interest to a wide range of Christian educators.

Catholicculture.org [www.catholicculture.org]

Offers insightful commentary on contemporary culture. Helpful for educators is their online library of scholarly—though accessible—articles on topics from politics to architecture to homosexuality.

Catholic Teachers' Guild [www.catholicteachersguild.ca]

A site of the newly federated Association of Guilds in Canada devoted to encouraging teachers in their mission as educators faithful to the magisterium.

Edocere: A Resource for Catholic Education [www.edocere.org]

Inspired by the renowned Catholic educator John Senior and under the patronage of Saints Thomas Aquinas and John Bosco, the site includes a host of helpful articles, an annotated reading list, and links to relevant papal documents. The site, it should be noted, promotes the SSPX.

Homeschooling Legal Defence Association [www.hlsda.org and www.hlsda.ca]

An important agency with American and Canadian branches, "established to defend and advance the constitutional right of parents to direct the education of their children and to protect family freedoms." HLSDA includes links to conferences and updates on legal cases relevant to parental rights.

Institute for Catholic Liberal Education [www.catholicliberaleducation.org]

Exists "to give Catholic educators a clear understanding of the riches of authentic Catholic education, yesterday and today, and to help them implement the Church's vision in their institutions." The Institute offers seminars and academic retreats for teachers whose schools wish to form faculty in the riches of the Catholic intellectual tradition.

International Center for Home Education Research [www. icher.org]

A center that "aims to synthesize the best of what homeschooling scholarship has revealed thus far, to examine new scholarship as it emerges, and to foster future work of the highest quality"; of note, their database of scholarly articles contains more than 1,800 entries.

Mother of Divine Grace School [www.motherofdivine grace.org]

An independent study program based upon the principles of Classical education, run by Laura Berquist.

National Catholic Educational Association [www.ncea.org]

An organization dedicated to promoting Catholic education in the United States. Helpfully compiles data on Catholic schools.

Seton Home Study School: Catholic Home Schooling [www.setonhome.org]

A homeschooling program with a highly developed curriculum. Homeschooling or not, many of the texts published through Seton are wonderful additions to the home library.

Sophia Institute for Teachers [www.sophiainstituteforteachers.org]

Founded in 2013 to renew Catholic culture through service

to Catholic education, the organization provides materials and in-service programs for Catholic educators across the country, linking prominent Catholic scholars with elementary and high school teachers.

The Cardinal Newman Society [www.cardinalnewmansociety.org]

Perhaps best known, and loved by parents, for their "Newman Guide" to faithful Catholic Colleges. The Site also provides access to their news reel, High School Honor Roll, and academic articles.

## H. Readers

Richard Gamble's *The Great Tradition: Classic Readings on What It Means to Be an Educated Human Being* (Willington, DE: Intercollegiate Studies Institute, 2009) is an excellent sourcebook of readings on liberal education. Ryan Topping's *Renewing the Mind: A Reader in the Philosophy of Catholic Education*, with a foreword by Don J. Briel (Washington, DC: Catholic University of America Press, 2015), focuses on the Catholic tradition, and includes a section devoted to readings on the contemporary renewal of Catholic education as well as study questions.

# Endnotes

[1] For background see Bradley J. Birzer, *Sanctifying the World: The Augustinian Life and Mind of Christopher Dawson* (Front Royal, VA: Christendom Press, 2007).

[2] Benedict XVI, *Address to the German Bendestag* (National Parliament), September 22, 2011.

[3] International statistics are gathered through the Organization of Economic Co-Operation and Development's *Program for International Student Assessment* (PISA). The PISA study compares educational outcomes among 65 nations including all 34 OECD member countries. For these figures see the publication *PISA* 2012 *Snapshot of performance in mathematics, reading and science* at http://www.oecd.org/pisa/keyfindings/PISA-2012-results-snapshot-Volume-I-ENG.pdf.

[4] See Anne Hendershott, "The Ambitions of Bill and Melinda Gates: Controlling Population and Public Education" in *Crisis Magazine*, March 25, 2013. The "Key Design Considerations" for the English curriculum (accessible at www.corestandards.org) notes that the 70/30 requirement does not specify the ratio to be taught in any specific English course, but rather the total reading distribution representing "the sum of student reading" in the senior year.

[5] Reprinted in Topping, *Renewing the Mind: A Reader in the Philosophy of Catholic Education* (Washington, DC: Catholic University Press of America, 2015).

[6] Such as, for instance, Mozilla's CEO Brendan Eich; see "Mozilla head's resignation over marriage stance sparks outcry" by Elise Harris in Catholic News Agency, April 4, 2014; or, among others, Philip Jenkins' *The New Anti-Catholicism: The Last Acceptable Prejudice* (Oxford: Oxford University Press, 2000).

[7] Stephen Wagner, "Behaviors and Beliefs of Current and Recent Students at U.S. Catholic Colleges" in *Studies in Catholic Higher Education* (October 2008).

# Endnotes

[8] John Paul II, "Ad Limina Address to Bishops from Illinois, IN, and Wisconsin" (cited in Miller, *The Holy See's Teaching on Catholic Schools* [Manchester, NH: Sophia Institute Press, 2006], p. 47).

[9] On Reginald W. Bibby's research methods and sample sizes see his Appendix in *The Emerging Millennials: How Canada's Newest Generation is Responding to Challenge and Choice* (Lethbridge, AB: A Project Canada Book, 2009), pp. 216–17. This study of about 5,500 15–19-year-olds examined students at 248 representative schools across the nation and gives us a fairly comprehensive picture of what teens believe and how they act. Most helpfully, the national data sets side-by-side kids enrolled in three high school situations: publicly funded public schools (at which attend 72% of the population), publicly funded Catholic schools (17%), and private Christian schools (9%).

[10] That is, 3–4% of the school-age population, or about 2 million, for each. For a brief history of Catholic education in the United States, and for statistics, see the website of the *National Catholic Educational Association* (www.ncea.org), the Center for the Applied Research in the Apostolate (www.cara.georgetown.edu), Curtis L. Hancock's *Recovering a Catholic Philosophy of Elementary Education* (Mount Pocono, PA: Newman House Press, 2005), and for homeschooling statistics, the *National Home Education Research Institute* (www.nheri.org).

[11] United States Conference of Catholic Bishops, *Renewing Our Commitment to Catholic Elementary and Secondary Schools in the Third Millennium* (Washington, DC: USCCB, 2005).

[12] For these statistics see Christian Smith and Melinda Denton, *Soul Searching: The Religious and Spiritual Lives of American Teenagers* (Oxford: Oxford University Press, 2005), pp. 41, 43, 47.

[13] Walker Percy, *The Moviegoer* (New York: Vintage Books, 1960), 207.

[14] Gail S. Risch and Michael G. Lawler, "Sexuality Education and the Catholic Teenager: A Report," in *Catholic Education: A Journal of Inquiry and Practice* (September 2003), pp. 53–74, at 63–65.

[15] These statistics are drawn from the National Survey of Youth and Religion and the National Longitudinal Study of Adolescent Health, discussed by Mark Regnerus in *Forbidden Fruit: Sex and Religion in the Lives*

*of American Teenagers* (Oxford: Oxford University Press, 2007), pp. 133, 139.

[16] See Smith, *Soul Searching,* pp. 210–11.

[17] See Frank Peters, "Religion and Schools in Canada" in *Catholic Education: A Journal of Inquiry and Practice* (March 1998): pp. 275–94.

[18] According to Bibby, 17%. See *The Emerging Millennials,* pp. 214–16.

[19] See the Second Vatican Council declaration *Gravissimum Educationis,* 6; Code of Canon Law 793.2; and CCC 2211.

[20] Reginald Bibby, "Restless Gods and Restless Youth: An Update on the Religious Situation in Canada," unpublished paper presented at the *Annual Canadian Sociologists' Association* (Ottawa, May 2009), p. 5. Available at www.reginaldbibby.com.

[21] See study by the Barna Group, "Americans Are Most Likely to Base Truth on Feeling" (February 12, 2002) at www.barna.org.

[22] See the 2012 PISA study *Ready to Learn: Students' Engagement, Drive and Self-Beliefs (Volume III)* (PISA, OECD Publishing, 2013) at Table III.4.2f (p. 310). http://www.oecd.org/pisa/keyfindings/PISA-2012-results-volume-III.pdf.

[23] See the OECD's publication based on the 2012 PISA study, *Snapshot of performance in mathematics, reading and science* at http://www.oecd.org/pisa/keyfindings/PISA-2012-results-snapshot-Volume-I-ENG.pdf. As it happens, Canadian students have slightly lower self-esteem by this scale, and achieve somewhat higher marks: 66% of Canadian students think they have good grades in mathematics, and Canadians score 13th on the same PISA international ranking.

[24] That was Pepsi Cola's four-million-dollar promotional slogan slung at our children during Beyoncé's multi-million-dollar promotional dance during a recent Super Bowl halftime show. Total U.S. media advertisement spending these days runs around 180 billion dollars annually.

[25] Some of these stats can be found on the USCCB's "For Your Marriage" Website (www. http://www.foryourmarriage.org/factsfigures/); for other statistics and sources see Ryan Topping, "Preparing for Your Marriage: A Bride's Checklist of Questions and Answers" in *Crisis Magazine*

# Endnotes

(June 21, 2013); and Waite and Gallagher's *The Case for Marriage: Why Married People Are Happier, Healthier, and Better Off Financially* (New York: Broadway Books, 2000).

[26] The Pew Center, *Modern Parenthood: Roles of Moms and Dads Converge as They Balance Work and Family* (Washington, DC: The Pew Research Center, March 14, 2013) http://www.pewsocialtrends.org/files/2013/03/FINAL_modern_parenthood_03-2013.pdf.

[27] This broad schema is set out in the Second Vatican Council's declaration on education: "True education is directed towards the formation of the human person in view of his final end [happiness] and the good of that society to which he belongs [culture] and in the duties of which he will, as an adult, have a share [virtue]" (*Gravissimum Educationis*, 1).

[28] For an orientation to the scholarly literature see the "Catholic School Advantage—Fact Sheet" published by the University of Notre Dame's *Alliance for Catholic Education* at https://ace.nd.edu/catholic-school-advantage/catholic-school-advantage-fact-sheet.

[29] For statistics see the report recently published by the Archdiocese of Pennsylvania, "Catholic Schools Save Taxpayers $2.28 Billion" (January 27, 2015) at http://www.pacatholic.org/catholic-schools-save-taxpayers-2-28-billion/. Nationally, the average cost to educate a child in a public school per annum is $12,401. With 1,939,575 students in Catholic schools that is a total savings to the public of 25.05 billion dollars. For the cost of public education see the National Center for Education Statistics at https://nces.ed.gov/fastfacts/display.asp?id=66.

[30] Oliver Goldsmith, *The Vicar of Wakefield* (New York: Pocket Books, 1961), p.64 (end of chapter 13).

[31] See his *Letter Addressed to His Grace the Duke of Norfolk: Certain Difficulties Felt by Anglicans in Catholic Teaching, volume* 2 (London: Longman, Green and Co., 1868–1881), p.250; quoted by John Paul II, *Veritatis Splendor,* 34.

[32] J.S. Mill, *On Liberty* [1859] (London: Penguin, 1985), p.69.

[33] *Nichomachean Ethics,* 1095a.

[34] Thomas Aquinas, *Summa Theologica* 1–2 q.4. a.4.

[35] For the speech see "President Obama Speaks at the Ohio State University Commencement Ceremony" at www.whitehouse.gov; for one intelligent commentary, see Brian Jones, "What Commencement Addresses Reveal" in *Crisis Magazine* (May 13, 2013).

[36] In Germany, some 32 colleges and universities existed prior to 1789. Roughly half were closed in the next decades, 9 of them Catholic. See Thomas Albert Howard, *Protestantism and the Rise of the Modern German University* (Oxford: Oxford University Press, 2006), p.135. For a history of the gradual descent in America toward an industrial, politicized understanding of education in the United States, see Charles Glenn's *The Myth of the Common School* (Oakland, CA: ICS Press, 2002).

[37] Richard Helmstadter, ed., *Freedom of Religion in the 19th Century* (Stanford, CA: University of Stanford Press, 1997), p.19.

[38] Letter of Thomas Jefferson to Tench Coxe, June 1, 1795, in *The Works of Thomas Jefferson, volume 8 (Correspondence 1793–1798)*, ed. Paul Leicester Ford (New York: G.P. Putnam's Sons, 1905), p.183.

[39] From D'Arcy McGee's June 23, 1858 address to the Legislative Assembly in Toronto, "The Separate [Catholic] School Question," in *1825–D'Arcy McGee–1925: A Collection of Speeches and Addresses*, ed. Charles Murphy (Toronto: Macmillan Co., 1937), p.160.

[40] Diary of John Adams, June 2, 1778 in *The Works of John Adams, volume 3 (Autobiography, Diary, Notes of a Debate in the Senate, Essays)*, ed. Charles Francis Adams (Boston: Little, Brown and Co., 1856), p.171.

[41] Rick Santorum, *It Takes a Family: Conservatism and the Common Good* (Wilmington, DE: ISI Books, 2005), p.335.

[42] Rousseau, *Emile: Or, On Education*, trans. Allan Bloom (New York: Basic Books, 1979), Book II, p.84.

[43] H.S. Gerdil, *Reflections on the Theory and Practice of Education Against the Principles of Rousseau*, trans. William A. Frank (South Bend, IN: St. Augustine's Press, 2011), pp.1–2.

[44] John Dewey, *Experience and Education* (New York: Collier Books, 1963), pp.19–20.

# Endnotes

45 See his article "Aims and Ideals of Education" in *Encyclopedia and Dictionary of Education*, ed. Foster Watson (London: Pitman, 1921); cited in William Kilpatrick, *Source Book in the Philosophy of Education* (New York: MacMillan, 1928), p.275.

46 O'Connor, "A Good Man is Hard to Find" in *The Complete Stories of Flannery O'Connor* (New York: Farrar, Straus and Giroux, 1988), p.132.

47 See "Who Knows What About Religion?," *The Pew Forum* (September 28, 2010) at www.pewforum.org.

48 This selection from the *Ratio Studiorum* taken from *Renewing the Mind*, p.212.

49 Isaac Newton, Letter to Robert Hooke, February 1676, in David Brewster's *Memoirs of the Life, Writings, and Discoveries of Sir Isaac Newton*, volume 1 (Edinburgh: Constable and Company, 1855), p.142.

50 Hilda Neatby, *So Little for the Mind* (Toronto: Clarke, Irwin and Company, 1953).

51 Congregation for Catholic Education, *The Religious Dimension of Education in a Catholic School: Guidelines for Renewal* (1998), p.25.

52 Shakespeare, *As You Like It*, II.vii. l.139–43.

53 This scheme inspired by John Senior's discussion in an unpublished essay, "The Integration of Knowledge: Discourses on Education."

54 National Endowment for the Arts, *Research Report #47: To Read or Not to Read— A Question of National Consequence* (Washington DC: NEA, 2007), p.9.

55 Newman, *The Idea of a University*, Discourse 6.1.

56 Aristotle, *Parts of Animals*, 1.1.

57 Hugh of St. Victor, *Didascalicon: A Medieval Guide to the Arts*, trans. Jerome Taylor (New York: Columbia University Press, 1991), Book 3.3, p.87.

58 See selections in Topping, *Renewing the Mind*, pp.277, 333, and 157.

59 Bibby, *The Emerging Millennials*, 201.

60 For a brief description of the document see Appendix 2.A.

[61] Archbishop Terence Prendergast, "Address to Wayside Academy," Wayside Academy, Peterborough, ON, June 8, 2013, at www.wayside-academy.com.

[62] For a review of recent research see articles in the Spring 2013 (volume 88, no. 3) special issue of the *Peabody Journal of Education* collected under the title "Reflections on a Decade of Changes in Homeschooling and the Homeschooled into Higher Education." The *National Center for Education Statistics* is the authority for the lower figure at 1.77 million or 3.4% of the student population. See http://nces.ed.gov/programs/digest/d13/tables/dt13_206.10.asp?current=yes. In Canada, the estimate is .4% of school-age children, or 21,662 souls; on this see Deani Neven Van Pelt, *Home Schooling in Canada: The Current Picture—2015 Edition* (Vancouver, BC: The Fraser Institute, 2015), p. 23.

[63] Brian Ray, "Academic Achievement and Demographic Traits of Homeschool Students: A Nationwide Study" in *Academic Leadership Journal* Winter 2010 (volume 8:1). For further research by Ray see the *National Home Education Research Institute* website, www.nheri.com.

[64] Deani Van Pelt, *Home Education in Canada: A Summary of the Pan-Canadian Study on Home Education* 2003 (London, ON: Canadian Centre for Home Education, 2003), p. 7.

[65] See D. Van Pelt, P. Allison, and D. Allison, *Fifteen Years Later: Home-Educated Canadian Adults, A Synopsis* (London, ON: Canadian Centre for Home Education, 2009).

[66] For research see www.hslda.org/docs/study/ray1997/07.asp.

[67] Benedict XVI, *Meeting With Catholic Educators* (April 17, 2008) at the Catholic University of America, Washington, DC.

[68] See "Address by Prime Minister Paul Martin on Bill C-38 (The Civil Marriage Act)," February 16, 2005, House of Commons, Canada, at: http://www.parl.gc.ca/HousePublications/Publication.aspx?Pub=Hansard&Mee=58&Language=E&Parl=38&Ses=1#Int-1132348.

[69] As reported in the *Washington Post*, "For Obama, gay marriage stance born of a long evolution," May 10, 2012.

70 Or, in more technical jargon, as Supreme Court Justice Anthony Kennedy, himself apparently Catholic, put it in the majority decision that redefined marriage in the United States: "The limitation of marriage to opposite-sex couples may long have seemed natural and just, but its inconsistency with the central meaning of the fundamental right to marry is now manifest," in *Obergefell v. Hodges*, 576 U.S. (2015), p.22.

# Image Credits

Chapter 1: *Madonna of Humility*, Fra Angelico, Italian, c. 1440, panel (courtesy of the Rijks Museum, Amsterdam)

Chapter 2: *The School Walk*, David Cox, British, 19th c., watercolor (courtesy of the National Gallery of Art, Washington DC)

Chapter 3: *St. Jerome in His Study*, Albrecht Dürer, German, 1514, engraving (courtesy of the National Gallery of Art, Washington DC)

Chapter 4: *Saint Cecilia and an Angel*, Orazio Gentileschi and Giovanni Lanfranco, Italian, c. 1627, oil on canvas (courtesy of the National Gallery of Art, Washington DC)

Chapter 5: *Geometria*, Hieronymus Cock, Dutch, 1551, print (courtesy of the Rijks Museum, Amsterdam)

Chapter 6: *Children of the Sea*, Josef Israëls, Dutch, 1872, oil on canvas (courtesy of the Rijks Museum, Amsterdam)